Ron Brown

Only Believe

Limited Special Edition. No. 21 of 25 Paperbacks

Ron Brown was born in East London in 1953. He went to a secondary modern school and left at the age of fifteen with very little education. About twenty years ago, he became a Christian and attended CLC church in Walthamstow, East London, under the ministry of Bishop Wayne Malcolm. He now lives in Birmingham with his Indian wife and their five-year-old twins. This is his first published work.

To my wife, Salomi; and our twins, Josh and Esther. To Berny and Simon, who helped me start this project; and to Delroy, who helped me finish it.

Ron Brown

ONLY BELIEVE

AUSTIN MACAULEY PUBLISHERS™

LONDON • CAMBRIDGE • NEW YORK • SHARJAH

A CIP catalogue record for this title is available from the British Library.

ISBN 9781528931977 (Paperback)
ISBN 9781528931984 (Hardback)
ISBN 9781528931991 (E-Book)

www.austinmacauley.com

First Published (2019)
Austin Macauley Publishers Ltd
25 Canada Square
Canary Wharf
London
E14 5LQ

Books that helped me with my research:

Smith Wigglesworth, Apostle of Faith
Baptized by Fire, The Story of Smith Wigglesworth
Wigglesworth, A Man Who Walked with God
The Real Smith Wigglesworth
Wigglesworth, The Complete Story
Greater Works
Smith Wigglesworth on Healing

And thank you to all who helped me with additiontional material.

FADE IN

INT. INSIDE THE LIVING ROOM OF 70 VICTOR ROAD. DAYTIME. MARCH 12, 1947.

Eighty-eight-year-old SMITH WIGGLESWORTH is sat in an armchair, wearing a hat and thick coat. He is waiting for a car to arrive to take him to the funeral of his friend minister WILFRED RICHARD.

His sixty-three-year-old daughter ALICE, who is totally deaf, is standing by the window in the living room, looking out onto the heavy snow-covered street. Turning her head slightly, she faces Smith to lip-read him as he speaks.

SMITH WIGGLESWORTH
(all Smith Dialogue with a strong Yorkshire accent)
Don't worry my dear, I won't get
cold. I promise that I'll keep my
hat and coat on all through the
service.

Alice beckons to Smith with a bigger smile that the car he is waiting for has arrived.

She helps Smith up from the armchair and they walk hand in hand, slowly making their way to the front door.

As the door is opened by Alice, ALFRED GREEN and his WIFE are standing on the door step waiting to greet them.

ALFRED GREEN
(with a big smile)
Good morning, I hope we're not too
early.

SMITH
(smiling back)
Not at all, your timing is just
right.

ALFRED GREEN
(also looking directly at Alice as he speaks)
We'll have him back in the warm in
no time.

SMITH
(squeezing Alice's hand a bit harder)
I'll be alright my dear, JAMES will
look after me.

EXT. OUTSIDE IN THE STREET OF 70 VICTOR ROAD. DAYTIME.

Smith is helped down the steps to a black saloon car with the Green's on either side of him.

They, then, help him into the rear seat of the waiting car. The car drives away slowly through the thick-covered snow streets by Alfred Green while his wife sits next to him in the front passenger seat.

EXT. INSIDE OF THE SALOON CAR. DAYTIME.

Smith is sat alone in the rear passenger seat looking out of the window.

SMITH
(looking forward as he talks to the Greens)
This is definitely the worst winter
I've seen in my life time… And I
am expecting this to be my last.

ALFRED GREEN
(ignoring Smith's last remark)
Let's hope they have remembered to
light the fires in the vestry.

SMITH
(sounding a little puzzled)
I was expecting everyone to be
coming to my funeral today instead
of brother Wilfred's.

ALFRED GREEN
(sounding more puzzled than Smith)
What do you mean?

SMITH
Some time ago, I was taken very ill
and was about to die. I felt that
my work for the Lord was not yet
finished, and so I asked him for
fifteen more years. He said that he
would grant my wish. That was
exactly fifteen years ago today.

ALFRED GREEN
Perhaps the Lord has something more
for you to do.

SMITH
(slowly shaking his head)
No, I don't think so. I'm sure he
would have told me by now. Anyway,
my spirit is still willing, but my
body is far too weak.

ALFRED GREEN
When did you first start to know
the Lord?

SMITH
That would be over eighty years ago
now, and I still remember when he
first spoke to me like it was yesterday.

Smith is looking out of the car's rear side window and his mind starts to drift back in time to when he was a six-year-old boy.

END OF TEASER

FADE OUT

Act One

FLASHBACK. EXT. A COUNTRY FIELD IN YORKSHIRE. LATE SUMMER. EARLY EVENING. 1865.
Six-year-old Smith is lying on his back by the side of the field, mumbling the Lord's prayer.

> **YOUNG SMITH**
> Our Father which art in heaven,
> hallowed be thy name. Thy kingdom
> come…

Smith's father, JOHN WIGGLESWORTH, is standing fifty yards away talking to a farmer on a horse and cart that is full of turnips.

Young Smith is still lying on the ground. His father calls out to him as the cart pulls away.

> **JOHN WIGGLESWORTH**
> (Voice at a distance.)
> Come on lad, stop the day dreaming,
> let's get on home.

Smith jumps to his feet and runs to his father's side. The two then follow the cart along a country lane.

> **JOHN WIGGLESWORTH (CONT'D)**
> (putting his left arm around Smith's shoulders)
> That's it lad, no more field work
> from now on.

YOUNG SMITH
(looking up at his father)
Why's that father?

John stops walking and puts his right hand in his pocket and pulls out a few small coins and shows them to Smith.

JOHN WIGGLESWORTH
That's why lad, not enough to feed
a growing family.

INT. LIVING ROOM IN SMALL STONE COTTAGE. EVENING. STILL LIGHT.
Inside the cottage, John, Smith and his younger and older BROTHER and younger SISTER are all sitting at the dinner table.

His wife MARTHA is standing around the table serving out the supper for them.

MARTHA WIGGLESWORTH
(speaking to John in a firm voice)
I still think he's far too young
for the mill.

JOHN WIGGLESWORTH
(replying in the same manner)
We need the boy to work.

MARTHA WIGGLESWORTH
Come on you children, eat up and
off to bed.

YOUNG SMITH
(putting his hands together)
Say grace first, Mother.

MARTHA WIGGLESWORTH
(changing the tone of her voice to a soft manner)

Alright dear you start us off then.

All the other children copy Smith by putting their hands together.

YOUNG SMITH
Thank you heavenly Father, bless
this food Mother has made, amen.

JOHN WIGGLESWORTH
(Looking at Smith bemused)
Who taught you to say that?

YOUNG SMITH
GRANDMOTHER says we should always
say grace before every meal.

JOHN WIGGLESWORTH
And what else did Grandmother
say…

MARTHA WIGGLESWORTH
(interrupting John)
She's asked if she can take Smith
to the service on Sunday… After
he's finished his chores.

JOHN WIGGLESWORTH
We'll see, now come on eat up, and
off to bed you children. We've an
early start tomorrow.

INT. CHILDREN'S BEDROOM IN COTTAGE. LATE EVENING.
Young Smith and his two brothers are lying on a double bed.
His younger sister, is in a single bed in the corner.

The children are watching a lark who has made a nest in the bedroom. A bird is flying in and out through an open window, feeding its young.

INT. BACK INSIDE THE LIVING ROOM OF THE COTTAGE. LATE EVENING.

John is still sat at the table, while Martha is walking backwards and forwards from the table to the sink. They are still arguing about Smith.

>### MARTHA WIGGLESWORTH
>The mill is such a dangerous place
>for a young boy.

>### JOHN WIGGLESWORTH
>He's a smart lad, he'll be alright.

BACK INSIDE THE CHILDREN'S BEDROOM. LATER.

The children start to settle down and go to sleep. The voices of John and Martha still arguing can be heard in the bedroom. Smith is lying in bed listening to them.

>### MARTHA WIGGLESWORTH
>(voice from the living room)
>He's still only six years old. I
>was hoping he could get some
>schooling first.

>### JOHN WIGGLESWORTH
>(voice from the living room)
>And how do we pay for that, when we
>can't even afford to feed him.

INT. MENSTON METHODIST CHAPEL. SUNDAY MORNING. 1865.

Smith is led into the chapel by his grandmother BELLA. About twenty five people are standing in a circle, about to start a praise and worship service.

BELLA
(holding up Smith's right hand)
This is my grandson Smith, and he's
come to join us.

An elderly woman makes room for Smith and his
grandmother as they join the circle.

INT. INSIDE OF WOOLEN MILL. DAYTIME. 1870.
Eleven-year-old Smith is loading a heavy sack of wool into a
hand cart. As he struggles with the heavy load, the MILL
FOREMAN and another MAN are watching him as they talk
together.

MILL FOREMAN
(calling to Smith)
Come over here lad.

Smith puts down his sack and joins the two men.

YOUNG SMITH
(taking off his cap)
Yes sir.

MILL FOREMAN
This Gentleman here, is the mill's
PLUMBER and steam fitter. He's
looking for a good strong lad to
work with him. I've already spoken
to your father, and he tells me
that you're capable of the
challenge… Are you lad?

YOUNG SMITH
Yes sir.

MILL FOREMAN
Good, now don't let him down.

YOUNG SMITH
No sir.

EXT. OUTSIDE OF A SCHOOL PLAYGROUND. DAYTIME.

Young Smith is walking past a school playground. He stops and looks through the iron railings at the children playing.

After a while, he takes out an apple from his pocket, shines it on his sleeve of his coat and takes a bite out of it. Smith, then, continues walking on kicking a stone down the street.

SERIES OF SHOTS.

1. INT. BOILER ROOM DAYTIME.
2. INT. WORKSHOP FLOOR DAYTIME.
3. INT. PLUMBERS WORKSHOP. DAYTIME. 1871.

Smith passing tools to the plumber while he is working on some pipe work in the boiler room.

Smith carrying the plumbers tools as they walk through the workshop floor.

Smith and the plumber sitting down, eating their lunch. The plumber starts to read his Bible to Smith.

PLUMBER
(with great intent)
There came a leper and worshipped
him saying, Lord, if thou wilt,
thou canst make me clean. And he
put forth his hand and touched him
saying I will, be thou healed, and
he was healed immediately.
(Closing his Bible and looking at Smith)
That's the key, you must believe
that GOD can heal you. You
understand that son, only believe.

YOUNG SMITH
(paying great attention)
Yes sir.

END OF FLASHBACK. INT. BACK INSIDE SMITH'S CAR. PRESENT TIME. 1947. DAYTIME.
Smith is still telling the Greens about his early life. They are both listening to him with great interest.

SMITH
I'll never forget that kindly man,
he taught me so much. And as well
as a plumbing trade. It was such a
special time for me.

EXT. FLASHBACK. OUTSIDE OF WOOLEN MILL. DAYTIME. 1876.
Eighteen-year-old Smith leaves his job at the mill. He is saying goodbye to the plumber.

PLUMBER
(shaking Smith's hand rapidly with a big smile on his face.)
Well lad, these years have gone
quick, and you've been a good
apprentice. I think you're just
about ready for the world now.

SMITH
(looking down sadly)
I don't know what to say.

PLUMBER
(shaking his head lightly)
No need to say a word lad, it's
been a pleasure.

Smith and the plumber hug each other and say goodbye.

SERIES OF SHOTS

1. INT. BEDROOM INSIDE OF HOUSE. DAYTIME.
2. EXT. COUNTRY LANE. DAYTIME.
3. EXT. OUTSIDE OF COUNTRY COTTAGE. EVENING. STILL LIGHT.

Smith polishing his shoes, putting on his suit and hat and coat.

Smith walking along a country lane in a happy mood, whistling. Smith approaches a country cottage. He opens the gate and then walks along the path to the front door and knocks on it.

Then after a short while the door is slightly opened. Half a MAN'S face can be seen on the other side of the door.

PLUMBING BOSS
(in a miserable voice)
Yes, what do you want?

SMITH
(removing his hat)
Good morning sir, my name is
Wigglesworth.

PLUMBING BOSS
Who?

SMITH
Smith Wigglesworth, I have just finished an apprenticeship and completed my time at Bradford woollen mill. I am now qualified as a steamfitter and plumber. I am looking for work in this field. Your good name was given to me and…

PLUMBING BOSS
(interrupting Smith)
No, I don't need anyone else.

SMITH
Well, thank you for your time sir.
I'm so sorry to have disturbed you,
good evening to you.

The man closes the door on Smith.
Smith replaces his hat, turns and walks away down the garden path. The man then opens the door again and comes out of the cottage.

PLUMBING BOSS
(following Smith down the path)
Wait a minute.

Smith stops. The man slowly walks around him, rubbing his chin and scratching the back of his neck and looking at him intensely.

PLUMBING BOSS (CONT'D)
Report to my PAY CLERK at 7 o'clock
tomorrow morning, sharp.

SMITH
Yes sir, thank you sir, goodbye.

EXT. WASHING AREA. COURT YARD OF A ROW OF HOUSES. DAYTIME.
Smith is fixing a tap to some pipe work. A WOMAN is standing behind him, waiting for him to finish.

WASHING WOMAN
Well, he said since you laid hands
on him, his back and legs feel much
better and he…

SMITH
(Smith interrupts by shouting to his MATE out in the street.)
Right turn it on.

Water rushes out from the tap that Smith as just fixed on.

SMITH (CONT'D)
(still shouting)
Alright, that's it.

WASHING WOMAN
Healing hands, that's what you've
got, that's what my old man said.

SMITH
It's nothing to do with my hands,
It's the power of prayer. If you
have faith and believe, then all
things are possible.

Smith turns the tap off. His young mate joins him.

SMITH (CONT'D)
(wiping his hands on a piece of rag)
Well that's it, that's the last
one, we're finished now.

INT. INSIDE THE OFFICE OF THE PLUMBERS WORKSHOP. DAYTIME.
Smith knocks on the office door. The plumbing Boss and his
pay clerk are inside talking.

PLUMBING BOSS
Come in.

Smith enters the office.

PLUMBING BOSS (CONT'D)
You're back early.

SMITH
(nervously)
No sir, the jobs all finished.

PLUMBING BOSS
You can't possibly be done yet,
There's at least another weeks work
left.

SMITH
No sir, your find it's all done'

PLUMBING BOSS
I'll not have shoddy workmanship.
I've a reputation to think of.

SMITH
Yes sir, I understand. I've done my
best.

PLUMBING BOSS
We'll soon see, I'll have to check
this one for myself.

INT. INSIDE A KITCHEN OF A SMALL TERRACE HOUSE. DAYTIME.

Smith as just finished repairing a burst pipe while the WOMAN IN THE KITCHEN is looking over his shoulder.

SMITH
(putting his tools back in a tool bag)
That should do it.

WOMAN IN THE KITCHEN
That was quick, someone needs to
tell your boss how good you are.

SMITH
(quietly speaking to himself)
That's exactly what I intend to do.

EXT. BRADFORD MARKET PLACE. DAYTIME.

Smith listening with great intent to a MAN PREACHING on a soap box to a crowd. Some of the crowd are jeering at the man and throwing fruit at him.

As he ducks from the objects being thrown at him he is trying to shout in a loud voice.

MAN PREACHING
And he said to them, go into all
the world and preach the gospel to
every creature, and he that
believeth and is baptized shall be
saved...

The crowd start to push and shove each other and a fight breaks out. Smith gets pushed to the ground.

The Preacher reaches out his hand and grabs hold of Smith's hand and helps him to his feet. The Preacher looks directly at Smith and continues to preach.

MAN PREACHING (CONT'D)
(Still holding Smith's hand)
But he that believeth not, shall be
damned.
(letting go of Smith)
And these signs shall follow them
that believe. In my name, they shall
heal the sick, cast out demons, and
they shall speak with new tongues.

Smith is standing still, staring at the Preacher as the crowd are still fighting.

Then a brass band starts to play, (WHEN THE SAINTS GO MARCHING IN.)

MAN PREACHING (CONT'D)
(in a calm manner)
I think it's time to move on,
follow me young man.

The Preacher and Smith follow the band as it starts to march away. The crowd continues to fight with each other.

INT. INSIDE THE OFFICE OF THE PLUMBERS WORKSHOP. DAYTIME.
The plumbing Boss is walking up and down in his office waving a letter about that he has been given by Smith.

PLUMBING BOSS
(speaking in a harsh tone to Smith)
(MORE)

PLUMBING BOSS (CONT'D)
And how do you think you will run your own plumbing business when you can't even write your own letter of resignation.
(taking off his glasses and speaking softer)
Now I'm a reasonable man son. I'll tell you what I'll do, you've been a good worker these last couple of years. I'll give you an increase of half a penny a job. What do you say to that?

SMITH
(with his head slightly
lowered)
I'm sorry sir, but my mind is made up.

EXT. BRADFORD CITY CENTRE. EARLY EVENING. 1877.
Smith is at a Salvation Army outdoor, meeting in the market_ square. A WOMAN SPEAKER standing on a soap box is preaching to a rowdy crowd who are throwing things at her.

Smith is standing next to a young girl in the crowd by the name of POLLY. She is eagerly jumping up and down trying to see and hear the speaker above the noisy crowd.

As she jumps up, she barges Smith with her elbow but she completely ignores him.

> **WOMAN SPEAKER**
> (ducking her head)
> The wonderful gift of salvation is for everyone who wants to receive it. Do you want to receive God's love. If so, then please come forward.

> **POLLY**
> (Mumbling to herself)
> Yes. I want it.

Polly tries to push her way forward to the speaker, but she cannot get through the hostile crowd.

> **SMITH**
> (removing his cap and speaking in a loud voice)
> Can I be of some assistance miss?

> **POLLY**
> (speaking to Smith in a serious manner)
> (MORE)

> **POLLY (CONT'D)**
> No thank you sir, I can manage on my own.

Smith ignores Polly's last remark and starts to push aside some of the crowd. Polly reluctantly follows Smith to the front of the speaker. Smith then stands aside.

WOMAN SPEAKER
(seeing Polly coming forward and stepping down from her soap
box)
Make way, let them through. What's
your name.

POLLY
MARY JANE FATHERSTONE, but my
friends call me Polly.

WOMAN SPEAKER
Well Polly, we have a meeting place
just down the road, where it's a lot
quieter. Would you and your
companion like to join us there.

POLLY
(looking seriously at Smith)
This Gentleman is not my companion.
(speaking in a softer manner to the woman speaker)
But yes, I would like to join you.

SMITH
(butting in the conversation)
My name is Smith Wigglesworth. If I
can be of some assistance to you or
the young lady, please don't be
afraid to ask.

WOMAN SPEAKER
Thank you Mr Wigglesworth, you are
also most welcome to join us.

Smith nodding his head in acceptance.

WOMEN SPEAKER
(speaking to a MALE colleague)
Let's move on before a riot breaks out.

The male colleague starts to urge the rest of the crowd who are not fighting to move on. Smith follows behind them.

INT. INSIDE OF KITCHEN AT SMITH'S PARENTS' HOUSE. EARLY EVENING.
Smith is sitting at the kitchen table, being served his dinner by his mother Martha.

MARTHA WIGGLESWORTH
(putting Smith's dinner in front of him and sitting down at the table)
Now tell me again what's her name
and everything you know about her.

SMITH
Well her name is Polly, and I don't
know too much about her just yet…
But I know I'm going to marry her
someday.

MARTHA WIGGLESWORTH
Oh Smith, how can you say that.

Smith finishes his dinner quickly and stands up and puts on his jacket that was hanging on the back of the chair.

MARTHA WIGGLESWORTH (CONT'D)
Now where are you going?

SMITH
I'm going to get to know her
better.

INT. INSIDE OF AN OLD WAREHOUSE. EARLY EVENING.
Polly and another WOMAN SERVER are serving food to a queue of homeless people in a warehouse.

Smith enters the building and starts to look around. Polly notices Smith and tries to keep her head down.

Smith still looking around, catches sight of Polly and makes straight for her. He then moves in between Polly and the woman server.

SMITH
(talking to Polly and tying an apron around his body)
Can I help you sister?
(MORE)

SMITH (CONT'D)
Shall I do the carrots or the potatoes?

Polly gives Smith a large serving spoon.

POLLY
(speaking to him in a uninterested manner)
You can do the peas instead brother
Wigglesworth.

SMITH
Please call me Smith... And I'm
quite capable of doing the peas as
well as the carrots and the
potatoes.

WOMAN SERVER
Well, I can see you don't need me
anymore, I'll leave you two to it.

The woman leaves them to continue serving on their own.

SMITH
(with a smile)
Well, we seem to have this under
control, don't you think so sister
Polly.

POLLY

Oh yes, so much so that you don't
need my help either.

Polly puts down the serving spoon, takes her apron off and
walks away. Smith stands there, looking bemused again.

EXT. COBBLE STREETS OF BRADFORD. DAYTIME.

Smith is marching just behind Polly on a Salvation Army's
rally. Polly is once again wearing the uniform of a Salvation
Army officer.

Smith comes from behind Polly and starts to march beside
her. Polly pretends to ignore him but then pulls up sharp holding
her left ankle.

SMITH
(taking hold of her arm)
Are you alright sister Polly?

POLLY
Yes I think so, but I must rest my
ankle a while.

SMITH
(pointing to the side)
Let's stand over there a while.

Smith and Polly stand to the side while the rally marches on.

SMITH (CONT'D)
Can you continue, or do you want to
rest a bit.

POLLY
(trying to walk)
I think I'll have to rest a while,
and then maybe go home.

SMITH
I can help you if you like.

POLLY
You don't have to go to any
trouble like that.

SMITH
It's no trouble, I'd like to help
you. Here, just rest your arm on
mine and away we'll go.

Polly takes hold of Smith's arm and they walk away in a different direction from the march.

Two male Salvation Army Officers notice them stop and look at them as they march on by.

SERIES OF SHOTS
1. INT. INSIDE A CHURCH. DAYTIME.
2. EXT. ON A STREET CORNER, BRADFORD TOWN CENTRE. DAYTIME.

Smith and Polly in a church service together. They are singing (ONWARD CHRISTIAN SOLDERS). Once again Polly is in the Salvation Army's uniform.

Smith and Polly are looking happy together as they stand on a street corner giving out leaflets to passes by.

INT. INSIDE OF MEETING HALL. EARLY EVENING.
Smith is sitting alone at the back of the hall looking sad. A SALVATION ARMY OFFICER approaches Smith with a letter in his hand.

SALVATION ARMY OFFICER
(in a sad voice.)
Brother Wigglesworth, I've got a
letter for you from sister Polly.
She explains everything in the

letter why she had to leave so
suddenly for Scotland. Would you
like me to read it to you?

SMITH
(holding out his hand for the letter)
No, there's no need. I know why she
had to leave so soon… My
intentions towards her were
strictly honourably you know.

SALVATION ARMY OFFICER
Yes I know. But when people start
to gossip, all sorts of silly
rumours start to spread. After all
she is an officer. And you, you're
not even a member. The army had no
choice but to post her out of
Bradford before a scandal started.

SMITH
I think I need to get away from
Bradford myself.

SALVATION ARMY OFFICER
Yes, maybe that's a good idea. A
new start somewhere else would do
you good.

EXT. BRADFORD RAILWAY STATION. AFTERNOON.
Smith is hurrying along the platform to a waiting train to
Liverpool. An ELDERLY MAN stops Smith to ask him a
question.

ELDERLY MAN
(holding a railway timetable in his hand)
I say young man, could you help me
and read out to me what time the

32

next train to Leeds leaves. This
small print is just a little for my
eyes.

SMITH
(angry at being stopped)
Do I look like the station master,
how should I know what time your
train leaves.

The elderly man is very shocked and surprised at Smith's answer. Smith feels embarrassed that he cannot read the train time table.

Smith realizes his answer is very rude and tries to apologies to the elderly man.

SMITH (CONT'D)
(feeling ashamed at his outburst)
Look, I'm very sorry sir, I'm just
trying to catch my train. I'm
afraid I can't help you, I don't
have my reading spectacles with me.

EXT. LIVERPOOL DOCKYARD AND SIDE STREETS. DAYTIME.

Smith walking around the slum areas and dockyards, looking shocked at what he sees. The people are dressed in filthy rags and many families are crowded into makeshift homes, cooking meals on open fires.

As Smith turns a corner, a crowd is gathered around two men who are fighting with each other. Smith makes is way around them and moves on.

A little further on, a DRUNKEN MAN with a bottle in his hand falls out of a doorway and grabs hold of Smith.

DRUNKEN MAN
(offering Smith the bottle)
Have a drink stranger.

SMITH
(trying to hold the man up)
No thank you.

DRUNKEN MAN
What do you mean, no thank you, my
drink not good enough for you.

Smith pulls himself away from the man and walks on.

DRUNKEN MAN (CONT'D)
(shouting at smith)
Hey you, come back, I haven't
finished with you yet.

Smith stops at a makeshift shack and knocks on the door. It is
opened by a MAN WITH A CAP on his head who invites Smith
in.

MAN WITH CAP
(removing his cap)
Come in young sir, please come in.

INT. INSIDE THE SHACK. EARLY EVENING.
Inside the shack, the man's family are all sitting around an
open fire, getting ready to eat their dinner.

MAN WITH CAP
Make way, make way, let the young
gentleman sit down. Will you eat
with us sir?
(Beckoning to his wife as
Smith sits down.)
Get another plate for the
gentleman.

SMITH

No thank you, I can't stay long, I
just wanted to know roughly how
many would be coming.

MAN WITH CAP

Well, so far it's about seventy, but
there might be more once word gets
around.

Smith stands up and puts his hand in his pocket and gives the
man some coins.

SMITH

I want to give you something for
all the help you've given me in
arranging this.

MAN WITH CAP

(taking the coins from smith)
Thank you kind sir, thank you
dearly.

Smith leaves the shack and walks a few yards further on. He
stops at a group of children playing. As the children crowd around
him, Smith talks to a SMALL BOY from the group.

SMITH

Hello, what's your name?

SMALL BOY

(in a quiet voice)

JOE.

SMITH

How old are you Joe?

SMALL BOY

                    (shrugging his shoulders)
              Don't know.
The group are joined by an older boy named SAM.

                        SAM
              He's four, I'm Sam, and he's my
              brother.

                       SMITH
                    (looking at the two boys)
              Joseph and Samuel, what fine
              Biblical names.

A small girl from the group of children comes from behind
Smith and grabs hold of his hand. Smith looks down at her.

                   SMITH (CONT'D)
              Where did you come from?

The children start to laugh.

                   SMITH (CONT'D)
              Make sure you are all there on
              Tuesday. There will be plenty to
              eat, and after dinner we'll have a
              story.

                        SAM
              Will you read to us mister?

                       SMITH
                    (taken by surprise and a bit embarrassed)
              Oh no, I'll be much too busy for
              that. Someone else will read to
              you.

INT. INSIDE A WAREHOUSE ON KEY-SIDE. MID-DAY.

Smith and a group of HELPERS are waiting for the people to arrive. Smith is pacing up and down looking at his pocket watch.

The rest of the helpers are standing behind tables of food waiting to serve the people when they turn up.

SMITH
(speaking to a bemused helper)
I don't understand, where could
they all be. They know what time we
are supposed to start.

The man in a cloth cap from the dock yard slums comes into the warehouse in a hurry and speaks to Smith.

MAN WITH CAP
I'm sorry sir but they won't come.
There's a rumour going around that
if they leave their shacks and come
here the dockyard, authorities won't
let them back again.

SMITH
(in an angry voice)
Why that's nonsense, the dockyard
authorities have given us this
place to help feed them.
(changing the tone of his voice and calling the helpers to him)
Right, here's what we'll do then.
If the people won't come to the
mountain, we'll have to bring the
mountain to them. Gather up all the
food and equipment and follow me.

Everyone starts to gather up the food and equipment, and they follow Smith as he leaves the warehouse.

EXT. SLUM AREA OF LIVERPOOL DOCKYARD. DAYTIME.

The people have finished eating the food. The children are sitting around in a semi-circle, listening to a WOMAN STORY TELLER with great interest to a story being read to them.

> **WOMAN STORY TELLER**
> (acting out the motion)
> And then David fired a stone from
> his sling at Goliath, hitting him
> right here in the middle of his
> head. Then suddenly the giant fell
> back and hit the ground with a loud
> bang.

She claps her hands loudly on the word bang, which makes all the children jump back with fright.

EXT. LIVERPOOL TOWN CENTRE. EARLY EVENING.

Smith and a small group of people are giving out tea and sandwiches to homeless people as they pass by in the town centre.

A HOMELESS MAN approaches Smith and grabs hold of his hand and shakes it hard.

> **HOMELESS MAN**
> Thank you very much for all that
> you have done for me.

> **SMITH**
> You're most welcome, have you had
> enough tea and sandwiches.

> **HOMELESS MAN**
> No, no… I mean yes, yes I've had
> enough to eat and drink. But you
> prayed for my arm last week when
> you were here. Look at it now, I
> can move it up and down with no
> trouble at all.

SMITH

Oh yes, I do remember now, it was
all twisted up from your elbow.

HOMELESS MAN

And I've remembered what you said.
From now on, I'll always believe.

The homeless man walks away. Smith is then joined by one
of the WOMEN FROM THE GROUP.

WOMAN FROM THE GROUP

I understand from sister Joy that
you have received another letter
from your young Lady in Scotland.

SMITH

Yes that's right, we're both
returning to Bradford to get
married as soon as possible.

WOMAN FROM THE GROUP

Oh Congratulations! That's splendid
news, I'm sure that you will both
be extremely happy.

SERIES OF SHOTS.

1. EXT. BRADFORD METHODIST CHURCH
   DAYTIME
2. INT. INSIDE OF 70 VICTOR ROAD. UPSTAIRS
   LANDING DAYTIME. 1873.

Smith and Polly coming out of the church arm in arm. A
group of people are throwing confetti over them as they walk
down the church pathway.

Smith walking up and down the landing. Suddenly the sound
of a baby crying is heard. Smith then enters the bedroom.

INT. INSIDE OF SMALL RENTED ROOM. DAYTIME.

Smith and Polly are talking to a BUSINESS MAN about renting a room.

> **BUSINESS MAN**
> (giving Smith a sheet of paper)
> Here's a list of the terms and
> conditions about the hire of the
> room. If you would like to read
> and sign it and let me have it
> back, you can start using the room
> as soon as you like.

> **SMITH**
> (giving it to Polly)
> Yes I think this will do nicely.

INT. INSIDE OF HOUSE AT 70 VICTOR ROAD, BRADFORD. LIVING ROOM. EARLY EVENING.

Smith and Polly are sitting at a table. Smith is struggling to cope, as Polly is teaching him to read the Bible.

> **SMITH**
> (reading very slowly)
> Fear… Thou… Not… For… I…
> (MORE)

> **SMITH (CONT'D)**
> Am… With… Thee… Be… Not…
> (stumbling on the next word and getting angry)
> Dis, may. It's no good, I'll never
> get it. It's too hard.

> **POLLY**
> (trying to encourage Smith)
> You are doing fine. It takes time,
> you have to keep on trying.

INT. BEDROOM AT 70 VICTOR ROAD. NIGHT TIME. 1884.

Polly has just given birth to a baby girl. Polly is in bed cuddling the baby as Smith enters the bedroom.

The FAMILY DOCTOR and a mid-wife are also present in the bedroom. The doctor takes Smith aside to talk to him.

FAMILY DOCTOR
(looking rather concerned)
Mr Wigglesworth, maybe it's a bit
early to tell yet, but we've done a
few hearing tests and your DAUGHTER
doesn't seem to be responding.

SMITH
What do you mean?

FAMILY DOCTOR
There might be a hearing problem.

SMITH
What sort of hearing problem.

FAMILY DOCTOR
It could mean that your daughter is
deaf.

SMITH
(in a proud manner)
That's nonsense, she can't be deaf.
Give her to me, I'll pray for her
healing.

FAMILY DOCTOR
Mr Wigglesworth, thousands of
babies are born deaf all over the
world.

SMITH
(Smith takes the baby from Polly and lays hands on her)
Not mine, I command that this baby
be healed in the name of our Lord.

The baby starts to cry as nothing happens. Polly stretches out her hands and takes her back from Smith.

POLLY
No Smith, we have a beautiful
little girl. If she's born deaf,
then there must be a reason.

INT. INSIDE OF SMALL RENTED ROOM. WINTER OF 1885. DAYTIME.

Polly is standing in front of a Congregation of about twenty-five people leading them in warship. They are singing (AMAZING GRACE.)

She checks the time by the wall clock behind her. Smith enters the room and bangs the door shut behind him.

The Congregation all look at him as he takes his place. Polly gives him a furious look as he mouths the word sorry to her.

INT. INSIDE OF KITCHEN AT VICTOR ROAD. EARLY MORNING.

Smith is sitting at the table, eating his breakfast. Polly is standing over him, pouring him a cup of tea.

POLLY
(sitting down at the table)
Will you be late again tonight
dear?

SMITH
(in a moody voice)
Probably.

POLLY

Do you know what time you'll be
back?

SMITH

No I don't.

POLLY

(looking at Smith)
It's just that you hardly ever come
to the services anymore. And when
you do, you are either late or have
to rush off because of all the
extra work you are doing on
Sundays.

SMITH

I have to do the work on Sundays,
I'm committed to it.

POLLY

Smith, we also have commitments to
the ministry.

SMITH

(Smith bangs his knife and fork against the table and shouts at
Polly.)
Commitments, don't tell me about
commitments. Do you know how many
people are relying on me to do this
work.

Smith stands up and grabs his jacket from the back of the
chair and then storms out of the kitchen.

**INT. INSIDE OF LIVING ROOM AT VICTOR ROAD
LATE EVENING.**

Polly is in the living room with the baby when she hears the
front door open and close.

She goes out to the hallway to see Smith at the top of the stairs, disappearing into the bedroom.

POLLY
(calling up to Smith)
I've saved you your dinner dear,
I'll have to warm it up first, just
give me a few minutes.

Polly starts to walk into the kitchen. Smith comes out of the bedroom and into the landing.

SMITH
(shouting down to Polly)
I don't want any dinner.

POLLY
(calling up to Smith again)
What's that you said dear?

SMITH
(shouting back down again)
I said I'm not hungry.

POLLY
It won't take long dear, just give
me a while and I'll…

SMITH
(interrupting Polly, and shouting even louder)
I said I'm not hungry woman, don't
you ever listen to a word I say.

Smith goes back into the bedroom and slams the door shut.
INT. INSIDE OF RENTED ROOM. LATE EVENING.
Polly as just finished taking the evening service, she is putting on her hat and coat and is getting ready to go home.

As the people are leaving the room, she is approached by a WOMAN FROM THE CONGREGATION who speaks to her.

WOMAN FROM THE CONGREGATION
Thank you very much for a lovely
service Mrs Wigglesworth.

POLLY
You're most welcome.

WOMAN FROM THE CONGREGATION
(in an inquisitive manner, with a lowered voice)
I was just wandering, Er… We
haven't seen much of bro.
Wigglesworth lately. I do hope all
is well with him. I know he is a busy
man but we do miss him so.

POLLY
(answering with a put on smile)
Yes all is well with him, and thank
you for your concern.

WOMAN FROM THE CONGREGATION
Oh well, I can see there's no need
to worry, you will pass on my kind
regards then?

POLLY
(trying to hurry)
Yes of cause I will. If you will
excuse me I'm running a little
late. Good night.

Polly rushes from the building into the street.

SERIES OF SHOTS
1. EXT. OUTSIDE OF BUILDING. NIGHT TIME.

2. INT. INSIDE THE KITCHEN AT VICTOR ROAD. NIGHT TIME.
3. INT. INSIDE HALL WAY AT VICTOR ROAD. NIGHT TIME.

As Polly leaves the building, she pulls up her coat collar and is singing to herself as she walks home.

Smith is sitting back in his chair at the kitchen table with his arms folded in a bad mood. He takes out his pocket watch to check the time.

Polly opens the front door of the house with her key and walks into the hall way. Closing the door behind her, she heads straight into the kitchen.

She is still singing to herself.

INT. INSIDE THE KITCHEN AT VICTOR ROAD. NIGHT TIME.

As Polly opens the kitchen door, Smith looks at her in a cold manner.

POLLY
(with a smile on her face)
Hello dear, you're early tonight.
As Mrs Dale gone home already…

SMITH
(leaning forward in his chair and interrupting Polly)
You're late woman, what time do you
call this then.

POLLY
I'm sorry dear, the service run
later then I'd expected and…

SMITH
(interrupting once again and raising his voice)
I don't care about the service, I
expect you to be here when I come

home.

POLLY

Yes, but…

SMITH
(in an angry manner)
No but, I'm the master of this
house and I'll not have my wife
coming home this late at night.

POLLY
(in a humble manner)
Smith, I know you're my husband and
the master of this house and I love
you very much.
(raising her voice)
But only God is my master.

Smith jumps to his feet and grabs hold of Polly. Opening the
back kitchen door he throws her out into the garden.

INTERCUT.
1. EXT. BACK GARDEN. NIGHT TIME.
2. INT. BACK INSIDE THE HALL WAY. NIGHT
   TIME.
3. INT. BACK INSIDE KITCHEN. NIGHT TIME.

Polly ends up on the ground, she gets up and dusts herself off.
She then marches around to the front of the house and enters the
front door again.

Once inside the house, she closes the front door and walks
through back into the kitchen again.

Polly is once again singing to herself. Smith is surprised to
see her and stands up again.

POLLY
(burst out laughing)
I'm sorry dear, you look so funny
when you're angry.

Polly sits down at the table again still laughing. Smith is still very angry and tries to grab hold of her.

Polly manages to slip free of Smith and he begins to chase her around the kitchen table.

Smith catches hold of Polly and throws her over his shoulder and tries to throw her out the door again.

With her legs kicking in the air and still laughing, Smith loses his balance and falls over.

They both end up on the floor pulling over a sideboard and breaking several cups and plates as it falls on them.

FADE OUT

END OF ACT ONE

Act Two

INT. INSIDE OF RENTED ROOM. EVENING TIME.

Smith and Polly are sitting down talking to each other after the service as finished.

POLLY
(in a serious manner)
Smith, this place is getting too
small. We can hardly move in here.
We need more room.

SMITH
Yes I know.

POLLY
But if we do take on a bigger hall,
you will have to devote more time
to the ministry.

SMITH
(in a humble manner)
Yes I know that too.

POLLY
And there's another thing. Before
we were married, you would never
raise your voice to me. But now you
seem to do it all the time. And
sometimes you have such a bad
temper too.

SMITH

I'm sorry, I didn't mean to hurt
you. I've been under a lot of
pressure since I took on all that
extra work.
(holding Polly's hand)
I promise I'll cut back at work and
spend more time with you here.

END OF FLASHBACK. INT. BACK INSIDE SMITH'S CAR AGAIN. PRESENT TIME. DAYTIME.

Smith is still telling the Greens about his early life as the car drives along through snow covered country roads.

SMITH

That was a very difficult time in
my life. I had become such an angry
young man. I could have lost
everything that was dear to me.

INT. FLASHBACK. INSIDE BOWLAND STREET MISSION HALL. DAYTIME. 1889.

Smith is giving instructions to two men who are carrying long benches into the mission hall.

Many other people are helping to get the hall ready for the opening service.

SMITH

(pointing to the floor)
Here… No this way round, that's
it, perfect. Now all the rest
behind this one in a row.

Smith's five year old daughter, Alice, is running around the mission hall with a group of other children. As she runs past Smith, he grabs hold of her and picks her up.

SMITH (CONT'D)
Hey you, slow down little one.
Don't you know it's dangerous to
run around like that.
(pulling her close to him and touching her ears)
Lord my pray is that one day she
will hear every word that's spoken
to her by me.

Polly walks past Smith carrying a vase full of flowers in her hands. Smith puts Alice down and she runs off again.

SMITH (CONT'D)
Polly, quick, come and see this.

POLLY
Smith I can't yet.

Smith pulls Polly along by her arm forcing her to put down the vase full of flowers on the floor.

POLLY (CONT'D)
Smith, Smith… The flowers.

SMITH
(still pulling Polly)
Don't worry about them,
Come and see what I got.

EXT. OUTSIDE BOWLAND STREET MISSION HALL. DAYTIME.
Smith still holding onto Polly's arm. He pulls her across to the other side of the road and stops.

He then turns around and looks up at a huge flagpole that has been erected outside the mission hall.

SMITH

There, look at that.

POLLY
(looking up in amazement)
Oh Smith, where on earth did you
get that from.

SMITH

Do you like it?

POLLY

It's so big.

SMITH

That's the idea, I want people to
see it from miles away. And I want
a big flag in bright colours with a
scripture on either side.

POLLY

What do you want on it?

SMITH

I am the Lord that healeth thee,
and on the other side, Christ died
for our sins. Come on, let me show
you where I want the same
scriptures inside.

Smith is still holding Polly's arm, as he starts to pull her across
the road again and inside the Mission building.

INSIDE BOWLAND STREET MISSION HALL. DAYTIME. MORNING SERVICE.

The hall is full of people who are talking amongst themselves.
As Polly takes to the pulpit, the congregation falls silent.

Smith is seated on the platform to her left, facing the congregation with a big smile on his face and his arms folded.

POLLY
(in a confident manner)
Good morning to you all. On behalf
of my husband and I, I would like
to welcome you all here to the
opening service at Bowland Street
mission hall. Let us open the
service in prayer. Would you all
please stand.

INT. INSIDE HEALING HOME MISSION HALL, LEEDS. DAYTIME. 1890.

Smith is attending a healing service. The SERVICE LEADER is praying for a line of people.

After the service is finished, the leader approaches Smith with two of his colleagues.

SERVICE LEADER
Brother Wigglesworth, myself and my
fellow ministers are to attend the
annual Keswick Convention this
year. And in light of our absents,
we are looking for a fellow
minister with experience to conduct
our services. We believe that you
are that man.

SMITH
(very nervously)
But, but I can't take your
services. My wife Polly does all
the preaching in our ministry. My
role is more of support, I'm not a
worship leader. I… I don't speak
well in front of people.

INT. INSIDE THE KITCHEN AT VICTOR ROAD. EARLY EVENING.

Smith and Polly are sitting at the kitchen table eating their evening meal.

> **POLLY**
> Oh Smith why on earth did you let them talk you into it.

> **SMITH**
> (looking confused)
> I don't know. I was tongue-tied, I just couldn't say no.

> **POLLY**
> Didn't you tell them how nervous you get speaking in front of people.

> **SMITH**
> Yes, of course I did.

> **POLLY**
> What are you going to do?

> **SMITH**
> (holding his head in his hands)
> Well I… I don't know.

INT. INSIDE HEALING HOME MISSION HALL. DAYTIME.

Smith nervously stands up from behind the pulpit. Clearing his throat, he starts to speak in a low tone to the congregation of about one hundred and sixty people.

SMITH (CONT'D)
(looking down)
Ladies and gentlemen, as I'm sure
you are aware… Or maybe you are
not aware, that your leaders are
away at the Keswick Convention.
They have asked me to stand in for
them, that is to say to take your
service… But I thought this
would be a good time for one you to
gain experience, by speaking today.
(looking up at the
congregation)
Would anyone like to share a word
with us?

The congregation sit in silence just looking at Smith.

SMITH (CONT'D)
Does anyone have a testimony that
they would like to give… OK,
then I think we will just have a
time of quite prayer.

Smith sits back down again behind the pulpit. The congregation sit in silence looking at him.

EXT. OUTSIDE OF HOUSE AT VICTOR ROAD. EARLY EVENING. 1890.
A well-dressed man in his early forties, knocks on the front door of the house. He is nervously playing with the rim of his hat. The door is opened by Polly.

POLLY
(greeting the man with a smile on her face)
Hello Mr CLARK, how are you?

MR CLARK
(in an anxious manner)
I'm sorry to disturb you Mrs
Wigglesworth, but is your husband home?

POLLY
(changing her expression to concern)
Yes he is, please come on in.

He enters the house. Polly leads him into the kitchen.

INT. INSIDE THE KITCHEN AT VICTOR ROAD. EARLY EVENING.
Smith is sitting at the table finishing off his dinner.

POLLY
(quietly)
Mr Clark is here to see you.

Polly leaves the kitchen and closes the door behind her.

SMITH
(putting his dinner plate aside)
Hello brother Clark, how can I help
you… Please sit down.

MR CLARK
(sitting down in a sad and gloomy manner)
I've just come to speak to you
about my dear wife. She's so sick
that the doctors only given her
just a short time to live. Would
you please come and pray for her.

SMITH
Yes of course.

MR. CLARK
(shaking his head)
We've been praying all night for
her, but nothing seems to work…
(looking directly at Smith)
Maybe my faiths not strong enough.
I simply don't know any more.

Both men stand, Smith puts his right arm around Mr Clark's
shoulders to reassure him.

SMITH
It's alright brother, go back to
your wife. I'll be along shortly.

MR. CLARK
The doctor said she'd be dead for
sure by night fall, she may already
be dead by now.

Smith opens the kitchen door and calls to Polly.

SMITH
Polly… Would you show Mr Clark
out please dear.

Mr Clark leaves the kitchen. Smith puts on his jacket as Polly
re-enters the kitchen again.

SMITH (CONT'D)
(taking out a cap from his jacket pocket and putting it on)
I'm off to see Mrs Clark. She's
seriously ill in bed and needs our
prayers.

POLLY
Will she be alright?

SMITH

I don't know. All we can do is to
pray for her.

POLLY

Are you going alone dear?

SMITH

No, I think I'll call on BROTHER
HOWE and ask him to join me.

EXT. OUTSIDE BROTHER HOWE'S HOUSE IN BRADFORD. EARLY EVENING. (STILL LIGHT)

Smith approaches brother Howe's house at a fast pace. The
house is a terrace house with no front garden.

Smith knocks on the front door. The upstairs' front window
opens and a man leans out and calls down to him.

BROTHER HOWE

Yes, who is it?

SMITH

(taking off his cap and stepping back to look up)
Brother Howe, it'' me, brother
Wigglesworth. I would like you to
come with me to pray for MRS
CLARK.

BROTHER HOWE

Just a minute, I'll be right down.

Brother Howe goes back inside the house. A few seconds
later he re-appears at the window.

BROTHER HOWE (CONT'D)

(in a joking manner)
What are we praying for this time?

SMITH
(in a serious manner)
Her life, she's lying on her death
bed.

BROTHER HOWE
(shaking his head from side to side)
Oh no I can't come brother, not me.
Please don't ask me to come with
you. There must be someone else you
can ask.

Brother Howe steps back and closes the window. Smith is left standing on the street bewildered at his decision not to come. Screwing up his cap in anger, Smith moves on.

EXT. OUTSIDE A SMALL IN BRADFORD. EARLY EVENING. (STILL LIGHT)
Smith continues to walk along the street to another house. Again Smith stops and knocks on the front door of the house. The door is opened by a man called NICHOLS.

BROTHER NICHOLS
Hello brother Wigglesworth, won't
you come on in.

SMITH
No time too, brother Clark as just
asked for prayer for his sick wife.
I'll explain on the way. Grab your
hat and coat and come with me to
the Clark's house.

BROTHER NICHOLS
(rolling down his shirt selves)
Oh yes of course, give me a minute.

Brother Nichols goes back inside the house. After a short while he comes out again with his jacket and cap on.

EXT. A STREET IN BRADFORD. EARLY EVENING. (STILL LIGHT)

Smith and Nichols start to walk towards the Clark's house.

SMITH

Now once we arrive, it's important
that nothing stops the flow of
prayer. Whatever happens I want you
to keep praying for healing for
Mrs Clark.

BROTHER NICHOLS

Yes I understand, I won't stop for
anything.

EXT. OUTSIDE THE CLARK'S HOUSE IN BRADFORD. EARLY EVENING. (STILL LIGHT)

Smith and Nichols arrive at the Clark's house. As they walk along the garden path the front door opens.

A DOCTOR, who is leaving the house in a hurry, leaves the door open behind him.

As he walks pass the two men, he looks at them and starts shaking his head slowly without saying a word. The two men enter the house.

INT. INSIDE THE CLARK'S BEDROOM. EARLY EVENING. (STILL LIGHT)

Brother Clark is sitting beside the bed on the right hand side of his wife.

She is lying on the bed with a white sheet pulled over her head.

Clark is holding his wife's hand pressed against his right cheek and is crying loudly.

There is a soft knock on the door, and Smith's head appears from around the door.

MR CLARK

(stops crying and looks up)
Please come in brother
Wigglesworth.

Smith and Nichols enter the bedroom holding their caps.
MR CLARK (CONT'D)

I'm afraid you're too late. The
doctor says she's already dead.

SMITH

(ignoring Clark's comments and pulling back the white sheet)
I hope you don't mind, I've brought
along brother Nichols to help with
the prayer.

MR. CLARK

No not at all, please make
yourself comfortable.

Clark stands up and offers Smith his chair, and greets brother
Nichols by shaking his hand. He then slumps down in a chair in
the corner of the bedroom.

Smith puts his cap in his right side jacket pocket. Nichols
stands at the foot of the bed.

SMITH

Will you start us off in prayer
brother? And remember whatever
happens, don't let anything stop
your prayer.

Nichols nods at Smith in acknowledgment and stars to pray.
But instead of praying for healing for Mrs Clark, he prays for
bereavement for Mr Clark and his children.

Smith tries to stop Nichols from praying, but Nichols takes
Smith at his word and doesn't stop for anything.

The two men are shouting as loud as they can at the same time.

BROTHER NICHOLS
(raising both hands above his head)
O' Lord heavenly farther, we pray for this poor bereaved man, and for their children who have lost a mother and a wife. We ask that you comfort them in this time of need and

SMITH (CONT'D)
(trying to shout even louder then Nichols)
No, no, that's not right, pray for healing. Stop this prayer, stop him Lord. We need healing for Mrs Clark.

Finally Nichols stop praying, then Mr Clark starts to pray, until Smith stops him.

MR CLARK
Yes Lord, hear my cry in this time of need…

SMITH
(turning to Mr CLARK)
No brother, it's your wife that needs our prayers. Let me lead the prayer, I just want you two to support my prayer… Lord we pray for healing and the resurrection of this body, in your holy name.

Smith pulls back the bed sheet that is covering Mrs Clark's body. He takes a small bottle of oil from his left side jacket pocket and starts to pour it over Mrs Clark.

Starting at her head and then all the way down to her feet. Taking out his Bible from his pocket, he starts to read it aloud.

SMITH (CONT'D)
And according to the book of ST
MARK chapter 11, verse 24, and he
said, therefore, I say unto you,
what things so ever ye desire, when
ye pray, believe that ye receive
them and ye shall have them…
Lord as we anoint this dear sister
in your holy name, we ask that you
raise her up again, amen.

Clark and Nichols look on anxiously, then suddenly Mrs Clark makes a sound of breathing out. Mr Clark stands up and moves closer to his wife.

The three men stand and stare at Mrs Clark, as once again she breathes out loudly.

This time she slowly moves her head from side to side and starts to mumble to herself. Mrs Clark then gradually regains conciseness and calls to her husband.

MRS CLARK
(reaching out her hand)
Is that you dear?

Mr Clark takes hold of his wife's hand and sits down beside her.

MR CLARK
(crying with joy)
Yes it's me, I'm right here, thank
God you're alive.

BROTHER NICHOLS
(looking at Smith)
My God man, you did it. You've
raised her, you've brought her back
to life.

SMITH
(sitting down in shock and shaking his head)
No, it wasn't me brother, this was
the power of prayer and the belief
of believing in miracles.

**INT. INSIDE THE KITCHEN AT VICTOR ROAD.
EARLY MORNING.**

Smith and Polly are sitting at the kitchen table eating
breakfast. Their two children, seven-year-old SETH and six-year-
old Alice are also sitting at the table with them.

SMITH
(with strong emotion)
If only you had been there, I've
never seen anything like it before.
She just woke up like being in a
deep sleep.

POLLY
(pouring Smith's tea)
I'm so pleased for the family that
She's alright.

SMITH
(with a smile on his face)
You know, I'd love to be there
today when the doctor calls again.
He's expecting to go there to sign
the death certificate, what a shock
for the poor man.
(reaching out to hold Polly's hand)

64

> Let's make a pledge only to rely on
> God for our health. We don't need
> doctors anymore, we just need faith
> in the Lord.

POLLY
OK, if you're sure you want to do
this.

SMITH
Yes I'm sure I want too

TWO WEEKS LATER.
EXT. INSIDE BOWLAND STREET MISSION HALL. SUNDAY MORNING. 1892.
Polly is at the pulpit, speaking to the congregation. Smith is sitting in his usual seat behind her.

POLLY
> Before we continue with the
> service, I want to tell you about
> the program for next Saturday.

Suddenly Smith gives out a yell and holds his stomach with his left hand. Polly turns around and speaks quietly to him.

POLLY (CONT'D)
What's wrong dear?

SMITH
(also speaking quietly)
Nothing to worry about, just a
stomach ache.

POLLY
(turning to the congregation again)
We will leave here at 9 o'clock in
the morning and march to the town

centre where we shall…

Smith fills a sharp pain in his stomach again. Crying out in pain he stands and staggers forward.

TWO MEN from the congregation rush forward and grab him before he falls. He is then helped from the platform and led away.

Polly looks on shocked but continues to lead the service at her husband's request.

SMITH
Don't stop the service, I just need
to lay down for a while.

INT. INSIDE THE BEDROOM AT VICTOR ROAD. EARLY MORNING.
Smith is lying in bed. Polly is sitting by his side.

SMITH
Don't cry. This is not a sad time,
but a joyful one. The Lord is
obviously calling me home. I know
we made a pledge about not seeing
doctors, but it's almost certain
I'm going to die, save a miracle.
You must protect yourself against
those who will call you
irresponsible. They will blame you
for my death. Now is the time to
call a doctor.

POLLY
(nodding in agreement)
OK, if you're sure that's what you
want, I'll call a doctor.

INT. INSIDE THE BEDROOM AT VICTOR ROAD. LATE MORNING.

Smith is being examined by a DOCTOR. Polly and a WOMAN HELPER are also in the bedroom.

> **SMITH'S DOCTOR**
> (Feeling Smith's stomach)
> How long has it been this bad?

> **SMITH**
> (wincing with pain)
> On and off, a few weeks now.
> **SMITH'S DOCTOR**
> You should have called me much
> earlier.
> (MORE)

> **SMITH'S DOCTOR (CONT'D)**
> I could have operated on you and removed your
> appendix. But now I'm afraid it may be too late.
> (speaking to Polly)
> I've still got two more calls to
> make this morning, I'll be back
> later to check on him again.

> **POLLY**
> (speaking to her helper)
> Would you show the doctor out
> please.

Polly's helper and the doctor leave the bedroom.

> **SMITH**
> I'll not let no man cut me with a
> knife. If it's God's will for me to
> die, then so be it. You've been a
> good wife to me and given me such
> lovely children. The money from the

67

business will take care of you and
the children, for a good many years
yet.

POLLY
(starting to cry again)
I wish we could have had more time
together.

Polly's helper re-enters the bedroom.

POLLY'S HELPER
There's some people at the door who
say that they would like to see
brother Wigglesworth.

POLLY
(wiping her eyes with a handkerchief)
Tell them that he is far too ill to
see anyone just yet.

SMITH
It's OK, I'll see them, show them
in please.

Polly's helper leaves the room again.

POLLY
You're too sick to see anyone, let
me go downstairs and speak to them.

SMITH
No, I'm not dead yet, there's still
breath in this body of mine.

The helper shows a small group of five people into the
bedroom.

LADY FROM THE GROUP
The Lord has directed us to come
and pray for brother Wigglesworth,
and to drive out the sickness.

MAN FROM THE GROUP
It will be all right Mrs
Wigglesworth, we can manage on our
own thank you.

The man ushers Polly and her helper out of the room. He then
stands over Smith and lays his hands on his stomach and pushes
down hard on him.

Smith let out a loud yell in pain. The rest of the group stand
around Smith's bed.

MAN FROM THE GROUP (CONT'D)
(In a forceful manner)
Spirit of sickness you have no hold
over this man, so we command that
you be gone.

Smith's body starts to shake. Slowly he stops shaking, and
then his body relaxes. He then puts his right hand on his stomach
and begins to rub it.

SMITH
(feeling for the pain)
Amen, I'm healed, that's it, I'm
well again. The sickness has gone.
I thank God for sending you all
here in my hour of need. Now that
you've done what you came for,
please excuse me. I need to get
dressed. I can't lay in bed anymore
as I'm no longer sick.

The group leave the bedroom and Smith gets dressed.

INT. INSIDE OF HOUSE AT VICTOR ROAD, ON THE STAIRCASE. LATE MORNING.

Smith comes down the stairs whistling to himself. As he is half-way down the stairs, Polly comes out from the living room. They both stop at the bottom of the stairs.

POLLY
(surprised to see Smith up)

Good God Smith, what are you doing up.

SMITH
I'm alright now, I've been healed.
While I was sick the Lord revealed
to me that you can't take anyone on
any journey that you haven't been
on yourself. I believe the Lord had
to let me experience sickness
first, to know what I'm up against.
And that nothing is impossible if
we believe in him. Now, since I'm
up and well, is there any work to
be done?

POLLY
(putting her hand in her apron pocket)
Yes, I've got a job that came in
yesterday while you were sick.

Polly gives Smith a piece of paper. Smith looks at the paper closely, and then makes a strange kind of sound.

SMITH
Emmmmm… I'll be home for tea.

Smith then kisses Polly on the cheek, winks at her, opens the front door and leaves the house.

INT. INSIDE OF HOUSE AT VICTOR ROAD, IN THE HALLWAY BY THE FRONT DOOR. AFTERNOON.

Polly's helper is answering a knock on the front door. She opens the door and the doctor is standing on the doorstep.

She lets the doctor in, and he starts to go upstairs. Polly comes out from the living room and speaks to him.

POLLY
Oh doctor, my husband not there.

SMITH'S DOCTOR
(Stopping on the stairs)
What do you mean, not there?

POLLY
He went out to work.

SMITH'S DOCTOR
(turning around and
walking down slowly)
Mrs Wigglesworth, your husband is
very ill. The condition he is in is
very serious. In fact, he is likely
to return as a corps.

Suddenly, the front door opens and Smith enters into the house. The Doctor looks at Smith in shock. Catching the end of their conversation, Smith speaks to Polly.

SMITH
False alarm dear, the job's been
done. Never mind, is there anymore
lunch left, this corps is hungry.

EXT. OUTSIDE OF HOUSE AT VICTOR ROAD. LATE EVENING.

Polly is looking out of the front downstairs window waiting for Smith to return. As he approaches the house, she goes out to meet him on the door step.

> **POLLY**
> (giving Smith a piece of paper)
> This message was left this afternoon.

Smith looking at the paper.

> **POLLY (CONT'D)**
> A young girl is very sick. Her mother says that she is desperate to see you. We tried to find you sooner, but you were not at the yard.

> **SMITH**
> (in a calm manner)
> Yes, alright I'll go and see her right away.

INT. IN THE BEDROOM OF A LARGE WEALTHY HOUSE. LATE EVENING.

Smith is standing beside a young girl who is lying still in bed. The young girl's mother and a house maid are anxiously standing behind Smith.

> **SMITH**
> How long has she been like this?

> **YOUNG GIRL'S MOTHER**
> Since yesterday morning.

SMITH
Has anyone else seen her?

YOUNG GIRL'S MOTHER
Yes the doctor has been here a
couple of times to see her already,
but he couldn't find anything wrong
with her. He said that he would be
back again tomorrow morning with a
colleague to see her again.

SMITH
(taking out his Bible from his pocket)
Would you be so kind as to leave us now?
YOUNG GIRL'S MOTHER
(sobbing into a hanky as she is speaking)
Yes of course.

The maid comforts the mother as they begin to leave the
bedroom.

YOUNG GIRL'S MOTHER (CONT'D)
(turning to Smith)
She has just been lying there
motionless since yesterday without
saying a word. We were so afraid
that we didn't know what to do.
Then we heard about your healing
ministry and then we…

SMITH
(Smith interrupting her)
Yes I understand, you did the right
thing.

The two women leave the bedroom.
Smith takes his jacket off and hangs it over the back of a
chair. Opening his Bible, he begins to read out aloud.

SMITH (CONT'D)
Is any sick among you, let him call
for the elders of the church, and
let them pray over them, anointing
them with oil in the name of the
Lord. And the prayer of faith shall
save the sick, and the Lord shall
raise them up.

Smith puts his Bible back in his pocket. He takes out a small bottle of oil from his other pocket.

He then pours a small amount in the palm of his right hand and rubs it on the young girl's forehead.

SMITH
(looking up)
Lord, I know that you haven't
brought me here on a fool's errand.
I know that you want this dear
child to live. Not by my might
Lord, but by Thy might, we ask that
you send your healing down upon
this child. In your holy name Lord,
Amen.

Smith sits down on a chair near the bed. Taking out his pocket watch, he checks the time against the clock on the wall, they both read 10:32 PM.

Once again Smith takes out his Bible from his pocket and begins to read it to himself.

INT. LATER THAT NIGHT.

The young girl in the bed becomes restless. Smith puts his Bible on the side table and then leans forward and puts his left hand on the girl's forehead.

Glancing at the clock on the wall, it reads 2:24 PM. Smith begins to pray again.

SMITH

Oh Lord, we need your spirit to be
with us now. This young child is in
need of your healing. We ask that
you touch her Lord and free her
from this sickness.

The bed covers suddenly fly down from the bed and the
young girl starts to shake violently.

Smith tries to pull the covers back and hold the girl down but
he is unable to do so.

The young girl starts to breathe loudly and then suddenly
stops and dies.

SMITH (CONT'D)

(gently holding the girls face and looking into her eyes)
Come out of her you spirit of
death, I rebuke you in the name of
the Lord.

The young girl starts to breathe again slowly and then opens
her eyes.

She looks at Smith and smiles at him, she then turns over and
falls back to sleep again.

INT. THE NEXT MORNING.

The young girl wakes up and gets out of bed. Smith is dozing
in the armchair, she shakes his arm gently and then he opens his
eyes.

YOUNG GIRL

Would you excuse me now please, I
need to get dressed.

SMITH

(standing up and putting on his jacket)
Yes of cause.

INT. INSIDE THE KITCHEN AT VICTOR ROAD. EARLY MORNING.

Polly is busy cooking breakfast, when Smith enters the kitchen.

> **POLLY**
> (turning to him in surprise)
> O' there you are dear. Just in time
> for breakfast. Come on sit down,
> it'll be ready in no time.

> **SMITH**
> (shaking his head)
> No, no I can't, I've a busy day ahead.
> **POLLY**
> You can't go to work like that, you
> must eat something first.

> **SMITH**
> (sitting down slowly)
> All right then, just a little.

Polly serves Smith some breakfast, as he starts to eat it, he falls asleep through exhaustion.

INT. INSIDE BOWLAND STREET MISSION HALL. DAYTIME. 13. FEBRUARY. 1904.

Polly is leading the congregation in song. Smith is sitting at the back of the platform facing the congregation.

A young man enters the hall with a man in his early thirties. The young man beckons Smith to him and whispers into his ear.

Smith then leads the man off into another room. On entering the room, Smith closes the door behind them and then invites the man to sit down.

INT. ROOM INSIDE OF BOWLAND STREET MISSION HALL. AFTERNOON.

SMITH

(pulling out two chairs from the table)
Now then, our young friend tells me
you need to speak to someone
urgently.

JAMES BERRY

(Sitting down in a depressed manner)
Yes, that's right.

SMITH

Let's start with your name shall
we.

JAMES BERRY

It's JAMES BERRY, and I'm full of
evil spirits.

SMITH

(in a curious manner)
You had better explain what you
mean.

JAMES BERRY

For nearly a dozen years, I was
chief hangman at His Majesty's
prison service. I've hung one
hundred and thirty-four people, men
and women. Some of them were
innocent as babes, and some of them
were guilty as sin. But all
convicted of murder and to hang. It
was my job to see that it was done
right. And all the evil spirits of
the murders were passed on to me when
I hung them. They told me inside my
head to kill myself to be free of
them. So I went to the railway

station to throw myself under a
train. Then this young man asked me
what I was doing, I told him
my story and he brought me here.

SMITH
Well I can tell you that you've
come to the right place. You need
to know that God doesn't want you
to kill yourself.

JAMES BERRY
How do you know that?

SMITH
The fact that he sent the young man
to you in your hour of need and
brought you here.

JAMES BERRY
But these voices inside my head are
so loud, they won't let me sleep at
night. The only rest and peace I
get is through this stuff.

Berry pulls out a bottle of beer from his coat pocket and holds
it in front of himself.

JAMES BERRY (CONT'D)
I drink so much of this at night
that I pass out, and I don't
remember a thing until the next
morning.

SMITH
Let me take that from you.

Smith slowly takes the bottle of beer from Berry's hand and puts it on a nearby table.

Smith stands up and opens the room door slightly and speaks to someone on the other side of the door for a few seconds.

Four men and two women enter the room. Smith gets Berry to stand up.

Everyone stands around Berry in a circle, with Smith facing him. Then they all lay their hands on him and Smith begins to pray.

INT. TWO HOURS LATER.

Smith is still standing in front of Berry.

Berry collapses with exhauster. They pick him up and put him in a chair.

SMITH (CONT'D)
(looking into his eyes)
You look exhausted. Let's get you
home.

Smith puts on his jacket and helps Berry to stand up.

SMITH (CONT'D)
Do you live far?

JAMES BERRY
No not far, at the top of Bilton
Place.

EXT. OUTSIDE BERRY'S HOUSE IN BILTON PLACE, BRADFORD. DAYTIME.

Smith, Berry and three of the men who prayed with them arrive outside his house in Bilton Place.

Berry knocks on the front door, it is opened by his eight-year-old SON.

BERRY'S SON
(shouting back inside the
house)
Mum, it's father, he's come home.

JAMES BERRY
(inducing the boy to Smith)
This is my eldest son, he's a good
lad.

SMITH
(touching the boy's head as he passes him)
Hello son.

The young boy holds the door open as Smith, Berry and the others all enter into the house.

INT. INSIDE THE LIVING ROOM OF BERRY'S HOUSE. DAYTIME.
MRS BERRY is sitting in the corner with a young child on her lap.

JAMES BERRY
(introducing his wife)
This is my wife and our youngest
son.

Smith and his colleagues removing their hats and saying hello to Mrs Berry.

SMITH
I hope we are not disturbing you
coming back like this.

MRS BERRY
(Putting down the boy and standing up)
No not at all, please come in.

JAMES BERRY
Mother, I've been freed of all
those evil spirits. I want to stop
drinking and to change my life.

MRS BERRY
(holding her hands to her face and crying)
Oh my God, is this true.

Just then Berry's elder son burst in the living room.

BERRY'S SON
(shouting loudly)
Mum! Mum! The delivery men are here!

MRS BERRY
(Looking at Berry in a surprised manner)
Oh my, I forgot they were coming
today. And I asked them to bring
some extra beer because you were so
depressed.

JAMES BERRY
Not to worry, I'll go and tell them
I don't want it anymore.

Berry puts his arm around his son's shoulders as they both
leave the room. Smith looks puzzled at Mrs Berry.

MRS BERRY
Once a week I have a barrel of beer
delivered here. It stops him going
out drinking and getting into all
kinds trouble.

Smith and his colleges follow Berry out onto the street.

EXT. BACK OUTSIDE BERRY'S HOUSE. DAYTIME.

Outside the house a horse and cart delivering beer is parked in the street.

Berry and his son are waiting as TWO DELIVERY MEN who are rolling a barrel of beer towards the house.

FIRST DELIVERY MAN
(stopping the barrel and looking up at Berry)
Now then Mr Berry, we don't want
anymore trouble like last time.

JAMES BERRY
No don't worry, there won't be
anymore trouble. I don't want you
to deliver anymore beer.

SECOND DELIVERY MAN
Aye what do you mean, you don't
want anymore. What are we suppose
to do with this then.

JAMES BERRY
You'll have to take it back. I've
been freed from the hold it had
over me.

Smith and the others standing around smiling to each other.

FIRST DELIVERY MAN
(talking under his breath)
There goes our overtime.

EXT. OUTSIDE OF HOUSE AT 70 VICTOR ROAD. DAYTIME. 1907.

Smith is walking along the road, approaching his house behind a MAN WITH A PAINFUL LEG hobbling along the road.

The man stops at Smith's house. Smith watches him pull himself slowly up the steps by hanging on to the railings.

He is about to knock on the front door when Smith comes up the steps behind him.

SMITH
Can I help you?

The man turns around sharply to face Smith and winces with pain from his right leg.

MAN WITH PAINFUL LEG
(speaking softly and holding his right leg)
Good day, is this residence of Mr Wigglesworth?

SMITH
Yes, that's me. How can I help?

MAN WITH PAINFUL LEG
(looking nervously around as he speaks)
I was given your name by someone who said that you might be able to help me…
(still looking nervously around)
Could we go inside please, I don't want to be seen talking to you on the street.

SMITH
(opening the door with his key)
Then you had better come inside.

INT. INSIDE THE LIVING ROOM AT 70 VICTOR ROAD. DAYTIME.
The two men enter the living room.

SMITH
Please sit down.

Smith's daughter Alice, who is now twenty-three years old, enters the room.

SMITH (CONT'D)
This is my daughter Alice.

MAN WITH PAINFUL LEG
(removing his hat)
Good day Miss.

Alice smiles back at the man.

SMITH
(talking to the man)
Would you like some tea?

MAN WITH PAINFUL LEG
No thank you, I'm fine.

SMITH
(looking directly at Alice and holding up his hand in a stop
motion)
I'll have my tea later.

Alice smiles again at Smith and then leaves the room.

MAN WITH PAINFUL LEG
(pulling up his trousers and showing Smith his right leg)
This is what I came to show you.
It's gone rotten with gangrene. The
doctor says he'll have to take it
off or I will die from gangrene
poisoning.

SMITH
(looking at the leg closely)
And what do you say.

MAN WITH PAINFUL LEG

If they knew I was here to see you
they wouldn't have me back. They
say you meddle with things too much
that don't concern you.

SMITH

If that's what you think of me, why
did you come here?

MAN WITH PAINFUL LEG

No, no, not me, I trust you. I know
what you did for Mr Lloyd's arm,
you healed him. Lay your hands on
me and heal my leg, like you did
for him.

Smith gets up and walks over to the window, he stares out
onto the street for a few moments. Turning sharply towards the
man he speaks to him.

SMITH

I'm not going to touch your leg.
But like Naaman, it's a question of
faith and obedience. He was told to
dip seven times in the river
Jordan. You must first go home and
fast for seven days and seven
nights.

MAN WITH PAINFUL LEG

(with a puzzled look on his face)
Is that all, is that it? I could be
dead soon. Why don't you lay your
hands on it and pray for me.

SMITH
If you trusted me enough to come
here, have faith that you will be
healed.

EXT. OUTSIDE OF HOUSE AT 70 VICTOR ROAD. DAYTIME.

Smith is inside the house looking out of the living room window.

The man with the painful leg comes along and climbs up the steps quickly and knocks on the front door. The door is opened by Polly.

MAN WITH PAINFUL LEG
(in a happy manner)
Good day, is your husband at home.

POLLY
Yes, please come in.
Polly steps back to open the door wider to let the man in.

MAN WITH PAINFUL LEG
No thanks, I'm in a rush. I just
wanted to show him my leg quickly.

Smith comes to the door behind Polly, then she returns inside.

MAN WITH PAINFUL LEG (CONT'D)
(pulling up his right trousers leg)
Ah, there you are. I just came by
to show you my leg. It's already
started to heal after just four
days, Isn't it wonderful.

SMITH
Oh yes, miracles are always
wonderful.

MAN WITH PAINFUL LEG
(moving closer to Smith and speaking quietly)
And when my leg is completely
healed, I'm going back to that
doctor and shove it under his nose.

SMITH
(laughing out loud)
So what are you going to do now?

MAN WITH PAINFUL LEG
First, I'm going home to finish my
fast. Then I'm going on a long
walk. After that, well I'm not sure
yet.

SMITH
Why not come along to the Mission
Hall and give a testimony when your
leg is healed.

MAN WITH PAINFUL LEG
(after a pause)
Yes why not, I think I will.

THREE WEEKS LATER.
INT. INSIDE OF BOWLAND STREET MISSION HALL. SUNDAY MORNING.
The man with the painful leg is on the platform giving a testimony about his leg being healed.

MAN WITH PAINFUL LEG
…And that's how my leg was
healed.

The man then turns around and looks at Smith who is sitting in his usual place behind the pulpit next to Polly.

MAN WITH PAINFUL LEG (CONT'D)
>And now I would like to show my
>appreciation to brother
>Wigglesworth for all that he has
>done for me.

Smith looks back surprised at the man and begins to shake his
head slowly in a no gesture. But the man continues to speak.

MAN WITH PAINFUL LEG (CONT'D)
>Brother Wigglesworth has expressed
>an interest about going to
>Sunderland, where God has poured
>his spirit out on his people. And
>they are now speaking in tongues.
>I have to attend to some business
>in Sunderland…
>>(turning to face Smith)
>
>And so I would like to invite
>brother Wigglesworth to accompany
>me on the trip there.

THE FIRST MEMBER OF THE CONGREGATION stands
up and speaks.

FIRST MEMBER OF CONGREGATION
>Is this wise, you know what is
>being said about speaking in
>tongues.

A SECOND MEMBER OF THE CONGREGATION
stands up and also speaks.

SECOND MEMBER OF CONGREGATION
>I've heard that it's the voice of
>the devil, and it's ungodly.

The congregation start to argue amongst themselves loudly. Smith sits with his head in his hands trying to hide his face.

Polly makes her way to the pulpit to try and calm them down.

POLLY

Please, please, calm down. There's nothing ungodly about speaking in tongues. God gave this gift to the disciples to empower them. As Christians, we need to explore this further. That's exactly what my husband intends to do.

INT. INSIDE A TRAIN COMPARTMENT. EARLY MORNING. 1907.

Smith and the man in conversation in a train compartment.

MAN WITH PAINFUL LEG

I'm sorry about announcing this trip to the congregation. I thought that they would understand and be pleased.

SMITH

(taking out a letter from his pocket)
Don't worry about it, I made the same mistake of writing to TWO BROTHERS I know in Sunderland. I told them that we were coming and the reason why.

(showing the letter to the man)
This is their reply.

MAN WITH PAINFUL LEG

What does it say?

SMITH
The usual nonsense… They strongly
recommend me not to come. They said
that speaking in tongues is the
work of the devil.

MAN WITH PAINFUL LEG
What's the matter with these
people, don't they read their
Bibles.

SMITH
Fear instead of faith, they are
frighten of what they don't
understand. Anyway, I need to see
for myself before I make any
judgement… Will you thank your
business colleagues for me in
Sunderland, for finding me this accommodation.
MAN WITH PAINFUL LEG
Yes of course.

EXT. SUNDERLAND TRAIN STATION. ON THE PLATFORM. AFTERNOON.

As Smith and his companion get off the train, TWO ANGRY
MEN are waiting for them on the platform.

SMITH
(walking with his head down trying to dodge them)
Looks like we've got a reception
committee.

The two angry men try to block Smith and his companion
from passing them, but they walk around them sharply and
continue to walk towards the station exit.

FIRST ANGRY MAN
(following Smith and speaking loudly to him)
Brother Wigglesworth, we were
hoping that you would postpone this
visit.

SECOND ANGRY MAN
(also following them)
These people are not Godly people.
We think that you should not mix
with them.

SMITH
Yes well thank you for your
concern, but I need to see for
myself.

The two angry men stop on the platform. Smith and the other man walk on.

EXT. OUTSIDE SUNDERLAND TRAIN STATION. AFTERNOON.

MAN WITH PAINFUL LEG
Well I hope your room is OK.

SMITH
I'm sure the room will be adequate.

Smith and the man shake hands and part company.

INT. INSIDE A HOTEL ROOM. EARLY EVENING.
Smith changing his suit in a hotel room.

INT. INSIDE ALL SAINTS CHURCH, FULWELL ROAD. MONKWEARMOUTH. EARLY EVENING. DAY ONE.
Smith is in a service with about twenty other people. The service is being taken by REV. ALEXANDER BODDY.

REV. BODDY
(talking to Smith)
And before we start, we would like
to welcome you to our service. If
you would like to introduce
yourself to us, please feel free
too.

SMITH
(standing up and speaking in a proud manner)
My name is Smith Wigglesworth.
But I'm sorry brother, I've not
come here to glorify myself but to
glorify God. And to receive his
spirit and to speak with new
tongues.

REV. BODDY
(surprised at Smith's reply)
Yes, well thank you brother, I
think you'll find we are all here
to glorify God… Let us all stand
and sing to God be the glory, great
things he hath done.

INT. ALL SAINTS CHURCH. EARLY MORNING SERVICE. DAY TWO.

Smith is in the early morning service looking bored. He is sitting with his arms folded looking around the church as Rev. Boddy is taking the service.

A man from the congregation is looking ANGRY WITH SMITH and is looking at him sharply.

INT. LATER. NIGHT TIME SERVICE.

Smith is having a heated argument with the man who was angry with him from the congregation after the service as finished.

SMITH

All I'm trying to say is I only
came here to receive his tongues.

MAN ANGRY WITH SMITH

Yes but first you must receive his
baptism.

SMITH

But I've told you many times I've
been baptized for many years now.

MAN ANGRY WITH SMITH

Yes, yes, but you don't understand.

Rev. Boddy comes over to break up the argument.

REV. BODDY

I'm sorry but it's late, and we
would like to close up the church
now.

EXT. OUTSIDE ALL SAINTS CHURCH. NIGHT TIME.

The man who argued with Smith inside the church follows
him into the street to continue their argument.

MAN ANGRY WITH SMITH

(in an angry manner)
Sir, I want you to know, that you
are by far the most stubborn person
we have had in our service. And
also for a minister who claims to
have a healing ministry, I find
your behaviour quite intolerable.

SMITH

Yes, but you see I was only trying
to…

MAN ANGRY WITH SMITH
(holding up his hand in a stop motion and interrupting Smith)
And further more we would
appreciate it if you keep your
views and opinions to yourself.
Good night to you sir…

Smith tries to talk to the man again but he walks away. Smith
follows the man still trying to talk to him.

SMITH
I'm sorry but you must have
misunderstood me, I was only trying
to…

MAN ANGRY WITH SMITH
(man stops walking)
I said good night to you sir.
EXT. MAIN ROAD IN TOWN CENTRE. NIGHT TIME.
The man starts to walk on but he and Smith both head in the
same directions as each other.
The man thinks Smith is following him, so he crosses over to
the opposite sides of the road and starts to walk faster.

MAN ANGRY WITH SMITH (CONT'D)
(looking over at Smith and speaking in a loud voice)
I'll thank you sir not to follow me
home.

SMITH
(speaking loud back to the man)
I'm not following you sir, my room
is this way too.

EXT. OUTSIDE OF HOTEL, TOWN CENTRE. NIGHT TIME.

Smith and the man stop outside the same hotel. They look at each other surprised, as they realize they are both staying at the 'same hotel.

The man takes out his door key and opens the hotel front door. Smith follows the man inside.

INT. INSIDE THE CORRIDOR OF THE HOTEL. NIGHT TIME.

Smith and the man stop outside rooms opposite each other. Smith is fumbling in his pockets, looking for his room key.

The man has opened his room door and is looking on curiously at Smith. Smith turns around and speaks to the man.

> **SMITH (CONT'D)**
> (in a humble manner)
> Sir, I find myself in a strange
> predicament. It seems that I have
> mislaid my room key. And as the
> reception is not open again until
> 7 o'clock, I have nowhere to sleep
> tonight...
> (speaking softly)
> Would you be so kind as to let me
> sleep in your room on a chair.

> **MAN ANGRY WITH SMITH**
> (with a strong sigh)
> This really is most irregular...
> (MORE)

> **MAN ANGRY WITH SMITH (CONT'D)**
> But I can see you are in need of a good Samaritan, so
> you better come on in. But I'll hear no more talk of
> your opinion.

Smith just holds up his hands and gestures silence.

95

INT. ALL SAINTS CHURCH. DAYTIME. DAY THREE.

Smith goes into the Church to see Rev. Boddy. The Rev. is in a prayer service in the vestry.

Smith puts his head around the door and decides not to disturb him. He then makes his way into the library to see MRS BODDY.

INT. THE LIBRARY AT ALL SAINTS VICARAGE. DAYTIME.

As Smith enters the library, Rev. Boddy's wife is sitting at a table reading a book.

SMITH
(In an apologetic manner)
Mrs Boddy, I'm sorry to disturb
you. I was hoping to see Rev. Boddy
before the prayer service started.
I must be getting back to Bradford
now. I've been here for three days
already, I have to go back and to
look after my own business. And I
wanted to say goodbye before I
leave.

MRS BODDY
(closing her book)
I'm sorry to hear that you're
leaving us so soon.

SMITH
(with a smile on his face)
Yes, I must go back now. I really
wanted to make amends before I go
for my rudeness last night.

MRS BODDY
(in a reassuring manner)
Brother Wigglesworth, I'm sure the
congregation won't forget you in a
hurry. But as far as making amends
goes, go and let the spirit of the
Lord go with you.

SMITH
(head bowed and in a quite manner)
That's exactly what I came to ALL
SAINTS for. I wanted so much for
the Lord to pour down his spirit on
me. I simply must have these
tongues.

Mrs Boddy moves closer to Smith and holds both of his
hands, with both of her hands.

MRS BODDY
It's not the tongues you need, it's
the baptism.

SMITH
(calmly)
My dear sister, as I've told many
members of your congregation, I've
been baptized for many years.

MRS BODDY
(shaking her head slowly)
No, no, it's the baptism of the
spirit you need. Allow God to fill
you with his spirit first, and then
everything else will follow.

SMITH
(kneeling down in front of Mrs Boddy)
Will you lay hands on me and pray
for the Holy Spirit to touch me
before I leave.

MRS BODDY
(placing both hands on Smith's head)
Yes I will. Heavenly Father, Lord
God, I pray that your Holy Spirit
will fall down upon this dear
brother, anoint him Lord, and
empower him to be your chosen
vessel. Let him carry your word and
your will to the four corners of
the world. Amen.

Just as Mrs Boddy finishes praying for Smith, someone starts
to knock at the front door of the vicarage very loud.

MRS BODDY (CONT'D)
Who on earth could that be knocking
so loud. Will you please excuse me
a minute.

Mrs Boddy leaves the room and Smith stands up again.
After a few seconds, Smith's body jars up straight, he begins
to shake, he then begins to mumble out of control and then starts
to speak in tongues.

**END OF FLASHBACK INT. BACK INSIDE SMITH'S
CAR AGAIN. 1947. DAYTIME.**
Smith still talking to the Greens as the car continues to drive
along snow covered country roads.

SMITH
I don't know who was knocking on
the door but I do believe that the

Lord had arranged it for me to be
alone with him as he filled me with
his spirit

ALFRED GREEN
What did you do next?

SMITH
I rushed back to the vestry to tell
everyone what had just happened.

ALFRED GREEN
And what did they say.

SMITH
Not everyone was pleased for me. I
think that they were more pleased
that I was going home.

ALFRED GREEN
How did Polly react to you
receiving the Holy Spirit?

SMITH
(with a smile on his face)
At first she wasn't too pleased,
but she knew that it was the work
of God and then she accepted it.

FLASHBACK INT. INSIDE THE KITCHEN AT VICTOR ROAD. EARLY EVENING. 1907.
Polly is in the kitchen with their eleven-year-old son,
GEORGE, she is reading a telegram from Smith.

GEORGE
Is that from Father?

POLLY
(holding the telegram
close to her face)
Yes dear.

GEORGE
(standing on tip-toes to see over his mother's shoulders)
What does it say?

POLLY
(mumbling to herself in an angry manner)
So he's been speaking in tongues as
he.

GEORGE
(impatiently)
What does it say Mother.

POLLY
(angrily putting the telegram in her apron pocket)
It says he's coming home tomorrow.

EXT. MIDLAND RAILWAY STATION. BRADFORD. DAYTIME.

George is waiting on the platform as Smith's train pulls into the station. As the train stops, Smith gets off and George runs forward to greet him.

SMITH
(putting his arm around George as they walk together)
Hello son, how are you?

GEORGE
Have you been speaking in tongues
Father?

SMITH
(with a smile)
Yes George, I have.

GEORGE
Can you say something now?

SMITH
No son, it's not to be taken
lightly. God will direct me when he
wants me to speak.

EXT. OUTSIDE OF HOUSE AT 70 VICTOR ROAD. DAYTIME.

As Smith and George arrive home, George runs up the steps towards the front door.

The door is opened sharply by Polly, who stands in the doorway with both hands on her hips.

As George darts past her, Smith makes his way slowly up the steps.

GEORGE
Look Mother, Father is home.

POLLY
(talking angrily to Smith and barring his way)
So you've been speaking in tongues
have you. I don't speak in tongues
yet, but I want you to know that
I'm just as much a minister as you.

Polly goes back into the house and slams the door shut on Smith. After a few seconds, she opens the door again.

POLLY (CONT'D)
And another thing, I've been
preaching the word of God for gone
twenty-five years now while you

have sat behind me on the platform
tongue-tied. If you're so full of the
Holy Spirit, you can do the
preaching on Sunday.

Polly slams the door shut again on Smith.

INT. INSIDE BOWLAND STREET MISSION HALL. SUNDAY MORNING.

Polly is sitting in the back row of the mission hall on a long bench.

The congregation are sitting in silence. Smith starts to makes his way to the platform.

An OLD MAN from the congregation speaks to Smith as he passes him.

OLD MAN FROM THE CONGREGATION
(in a sarcastic manner)
What are you going to preach about
son?

SMITH
(walking past the old man)
The word of God.
Smith on the platform and facing the congregation.

SMITH (CONT'D)
(opening his Bible and reading with great authority)
The spirit of the Lord is upon me,
because the Lord hath anointed me
to preach good tidings unto the
meek, he hath sent me to bind up
the broken-hearted, to proclaim
liberty to the captives, and the
opening of the prison to them that
are bound. To proclaim the
acceptable year of the Lord.
(looking at the congregation)

Brothers, sisters, are you meek.

Polly is sliding up and down on the bench so much that it is disturbing those at the back of the hall.

POLLY
(speaking to herself loudly)
That's not my Smith, that can't be
him… He's preaching so well.

SMITH
Are you broken-hearted, are you
captives, or are you just
bound…

POLLY
(still speaking to herself)
That's amazing, where did he get
that confidence to speak like that.

INT. MISSION HALL. TWO HOURS LATER.
Smith is about to finish his sermon, after two hours of preaching. Polly is still sliding up and down on the bench, and still talking to herself.
POLLY (CONT'D)
(in amazement)
I've never heard him speak like
that before.

SMITH
(closing his Bible and holding it up in the air)
And finally brothers and sisters,
let me tell you the answer to this.
It is to believe this book with all
your heart… Only believe… Amen.

As Smith leaves the platform, a well-dressed man from the congregation stands up to speak to Smith.

WELL DRESSED MAN
You say brother Wigglesworth that
when you received the Holy Spirit,
you began to speak in new tongues.

SMITH
Yes that's correct brother.

WELL DRESSED MAN
(very nervously)
I was wondering, er… well, we were
wondering, that's me and some of
the congregation, if we could hear
some of these tongues.

Smith turns around and returns to the platform.

SMITH
(opening his Bible)
Please open your Bibles at 1
CORINTHIANS 14, VERSE 19. And I
read the words of our beloved
apostle Paul. Yct in the church I
had rather speak five words with my
understanding, that by my voice I
might teach others also, then ten
thousand words in an unknown
tongue.
(holding his Bible in his right hand and pointing it towards the
congregation)
(MORE)

SMITH (CONT'D)
And why do you think that Paul spoke these words…
(putting his Bible down)
Paul knew that if the whole church
turned to tongues, and tongues
only, there would be confusion and

there would not be a lift of divine
power and fellowship that was much
needed. When God speaks to the
church, his words of wisdom are to
be understood.
(pointing his finger at the congregation)
Who among you can interpret these
tongues?

EXT. A SMALL MINING VILLAGE IN SOUTH WALES. LATE AFTERNOON.

Smith and a friend are walking along the main road in the village. As they approach a grocers shop they stop.

Smith takes out a piece of paper from his pocket and looks at it.

SMITH
(talking to his friend)
This looks like the shop.

The two men enter the shop.

INT. INSIDE A VILLAGE GROCER'S SHOP. LATE AFTERNOON.

Behind the counter is a GROCER in his early fifties. An ELDERLY COUPLE are also in the shop.

GROCER
(with a smile)
Good day gentlemen, how can I help
you?

SMITH
(removing his hat)
Good day sir, my name is
Wigglesworth, Smith Wigglesworth. I
sent you a postcard about your
local minister. His name is

LAZARUS, and we're here to raise
him up again.

The Grocer takes out a post card from under the counter and
throws it down on top of the counter in front of Smith.
Folding his arms, he speaks to Smith in an angry manner.

GROCER
What makes you think that he wants
to be raised up again?

SMITH
What makes you think that he
doesn't?

GROCER
He's nearer his death bed than
being raised. Anyway what makes you
think we believe in this sort of
thing.

SMITH
(smiling at the man)
Don't worry brother, I've enough
belief for all of us. Can we see
him?

GROCER
(still angry with Smith)
No that won't be possible now. He
always rests in the afternoon.
You'll have to come back tomorrow
if you want to see him.

SMITH
Is there anywhere we can stay for
the night in the village?

GROCER
(shaking his head)
No, I'm afraid not, there's no one
who can help you here.

SMITH
Oh well, thank you for your time.

Smith and his friend leave the shop.

EXT. OUTSIDE THE VILLAGE GROCERS SHOP. LATE AFTERNOON.

Smith and his friend are followed outside the shop by the elderly couple who speak to them.

ELDERLY LADY
Excuse me, he's wrong you know.
We can help you.
(MORE)

ELDERLY LADY (CONT'D)
And there are people in this village who would like to
see Lazarus raised up again.

SMITH
Thank you kindly madam. Can you
tell us if there is anywhere in the
village where we could stay for the
night.

ELDERLY LADY
If you don't mind sharing a small
room you are welcome to stay with
us for the night.

The elderly gentleman nods in agreement.

INT. INSIDE A LIVING ROOM OF A HOUSE. LATE EVENING.

Smith, his friend and the elderly couple are sitting around a table in the living room.

SMITH
Why is the Grocer so against us,
doesn't he want to see Lazarus well
again.

ELDERLY LADY
I think that he feels his position
as head man in the village is
threatened, if Lazarus is raised
again.

ELDERLY GENTLEMAN
We tried to keep the ministry going
when he became ill, but it was just
too hard for us.

SMITH
Can we get some more people to help
with the prayers tomorrow.

ELDERLY GENTLEMAN
Yes I think so, we should be able
to get three or four more to help
us.

SMITH
Good, now I think it's time we
retire. Good night to you.

Smith and his friend stand up and leave the room.

INT. INSIDE A BEDROOM IN THE HOUSE. NIGHT TIME.

Smith and his friend are sharing a double bed in the room. Both men are sleeping fully clothed on top of the bed.

INT. BACK INSIDE THE LIVING ROOM OF THE HOUSE. EARLY MORNING.

Smith, his friend and the elderly couple are all sitting around the living room table.

ELDERLY LADY
(standing to serve tea)
Will you have some tea brother
Wigglesworth, it's so refreshing.

SMITH
No thank you sister. There's
nothing more refreshing than
fasting.
(looking at his pocket watch)
I think it's time we made a move.

EXT. THE MAIN STREET IN THE VILLAGE. MORNING TIME.

Smith, his friend and the elderly couple are walking along the road towards Lazarus' house in a single file.

With Smith at the head, they are soon joined at the rear by two men and a women.

EXT. OUTSIDE LAZARUS'S HOUSE. MORNING TIME.

As they approach Lazarus's house, people in the village stare at them.

The grocer and a small group of men are also standing outside Lazarus' house on the front door step blocking Smith's way.

GROCER
(with his arms folded)
Once you see the condition he is in,

you will soon change your mind and
move on.

SMITH
I'm not moved by what I see, only
by what I believe.

The group of men are still blocking Smith's way.

GROCER
Why have you come here poking your
nose into our business. If you want
your God to heal someone, you
should ask him to heal your own
first.

SMITH
Please explain yourself sir.

GROCER
We know you're that Minister who has a deaf
daughter.

SMITH
That's true sir, but because she
was born that way, it must mean
that God did not think it was
necessary for her to hear.

Smith tries again to push his way past the Grocer and the other
group of men, but they are still blocking the entrance to the house.

SMITH (CONT'D)
(standing back and shouting with a loud voice)
Lazarus, rise in the name of our
Lord.

GROCER
(laughing loudly and shouting at Smith)
He's not rising for anybody. He's
been bedridden for too long.

The group of men with the grocer also start to laugh at Smith.
After a short while, the front door of the house slowly starts
to open and Lazarus appears on the door step.

The grocer and the group of men with him start to turn around
and then stop laughing and look at Lazarus in surprise.

END OF FLASHBACK. EXT. BACK INSIDE SMITH'S CAR. PRESENT TIME. DAYTIME. MARCH 12. 1947.
'   Smith still talking to the Greens.

SMITH
(with a big smile on his face)
Once again Lazarus had been raised,
and just like the first time many
people came from miles around to
see him. But not everyone believed
he had been raised up again. Some
didn't believe that there was a
sickness to start with…
Particularly one gentleman from the
press who started to attend the
healing services that I was
conducting.

FLASHBACK. EXT. IN A FACTORY YARD IN BRADFORD. 1912. DAYTIME.
Smith is talking to two men in a factory yard. The men are
wearing sandwich boards advertising a banquet at Bowland
Street Mission Hall.

SMITH
Now don't forget to tell them that
everything is free, and that there
will be entertainment provided as
well. And let me know as soon as
you can how many will need help
coming.

The two men nod in agreement and walk away.

INT. INSIDE THE KITCHEN AT VICTOR ROAD. MORNING TIME.
Smith is sitting at the kitchen table looking at several pieces
of paper with names and addresses on them.

SMITH
(standing up sharply and talking to himself)
This one will do me.

Smith puts on his jacket and then calls out to Polly in the next
room through the slightly opened door.
SMITH (CONT'D)
I'm off now, see you later, bye.

POLLY
(voice in the next room)
Bye dear, have fun.

Smith leaves the kitchen through the back door.

INT. INSIDE A HOUSE LIVING ROOM IN BRADFORD. MORNING TIME.
Smith is talking to an elderly FRAIL LADY while he is
kneeling down on the floor re-fixing a wheel back onto a wheel
chair.

SMITH

(spinning the wheel of the chair)
That should hold it for now.
(standing up and putting on his jacket)
Come on sister let's get you to the
banquet.

EXT. OUTSIDE ON THE STREET IN BRADFORD. MORNING TIME.

Smith is pushing the wheel chair along the road with the frail lady in it.

They are both singing as they make their way to the mission hall. The wheel that Smith repaired earlier on, comes off the chair again.

As the wheel breaks off, it rolls away down the street. Smith keeps on pushing the chair along the road, but has to support one side to stop the frail lady falling out.

SMITH

(stopping briefly)
Sister, if the good Lord has
allowed the wheel to break away
again, it must mean you won't need the chair after
today.

Smith continues to push the chair again and the two carry on singing as they make their way to the mission hall.

INT. INSIDE OF BOWLAND STREET MISSION HALL. MIDDAY.

The mission hall is full of people who are all seated around tables and have just finished a meal. Smith is standing in the aisle talking to Polly.

SMITH

I'm so pleased we've had a good
turn out. But now that the food is
finished, we need to keep their

interest going or they will all
disappear.

POLLY
Speaking of interest, we have a
LOCAL REPORTER here today. He said
that he would like to speak to you.

SMITH
Yes well, I'm sure he'll find me
later. Right now I need to be up on
the platform.

Smith makes his way up to the platform.

SMITH (CONT'D)
I hope you've all enjoyed your
meal. And now it's time for the
testimonies to start.

Smith beckons to a group of people to join him on the
platform. The group are led by a man named JACOB.

SMITH
While we wait for brother Jacob and
the others to bring us their
testimonies. I want to tell you
that you are all welcome back here
tomorrow for our morning service.
(turning to brother Jacob)
Would you like to start us off
brother?

BROTHER JACOBS
For many years I had been bound in
a wheel chair. I was told that God
could heal me through the power of
prayer by a neighbour. So I came
along here to see brother

Wigglesworth, and he laid hands on
me and prayed for me. As you can
see, my prayers were answered.

The crowd start to clap and cheer. Standing by the front of the platform leaning against the wall, a man from the press is taking notes in a notebook.

                         SMITH
                  (quieting them down again)
            Thank you, thank you… Thank you
            brother.
                  (turning to a woman)
            You're next sister.

                WOMAN ON PLATFORM
                  (very nervously)
            Thank you brother Wigglesworth.
                  (MORE)

            WOMAN ON PLATFORM (CONT'D)
            Just like the woman in the Bible, I had an issue of
            blood. I was due to be admitted to hospital for my
            condition. Brother Wigglesworth anointed me with oil
            and laid hands on me and prayed for my healing and
            God healed me.

Once again the crowd clap and cheer. Smith notices the man taking notes. The man looks at Smith and nods his head at him in recognition.

                         SMITH
                  (raising his hands again)
            Thank you, thank you once again.
                  (turning to the woman)
            And thank you sister for your
            testimony. Who do we have next.

INT. MISSION HALL. HALF AN HOUR LATER.

Smith is still on the platform with the last person to give her testimony.

SMITH
(turning to the women)
And finally SISTER, tell us your
story of healing.

SISTER ON PLATFORM
I was in so much pain in my back
and legs that I could only stand
for a few minutes at a time. The
doctors could not find anything
wrong with me. They all said that
it was probably down to my age and
that there was nothing that could
be done.
(turning to Smith)
Brother Wigglesworth laid hands on
me and prayed for my healing. As
you can see, I've been standing
here for half an hour already.

Once again the crowd cheer as the sister leaves the platform.

SMITH
And now I'm going to invite SISTER
MAY and her brother JOHN to come up
to the platform and sing for us.

Sister May and her brother John, with his guitar come up to the platform.

Smith leaves the platform and re-joins Polly. A LOCAL REPORTER approaches them and speaks to Smith.

SISTER MAY

(singing in the back ground)
My Lord he asks me, just to
love him. He knows that I do
adore him. I'll praise his
name with all the glory. Yes
I'll praise his name with all
the glory. And in return
he'll give to me his grace
and love for all to see. Yes
in return I know he'll be, a
mighty God who cares for me.
My Lord he asks me, to tell
his story. His power, his
love, his might and glory. My
love for him will not desert
me. Yes my love for him will
not desert me. And in return
he'll give to me, his grace
and love for all to see. Yes
in return I know he'll be, a
mighty God who cares for me.

LOCAL REPORTER

MR WIGGLESWORTH, I've been
having some interesting
conversations with some of
the people here tonight. They
are telling me of all sorts
of strange healings they
clam to have taken place…
Do you know that some experts
in the medical field believe
that through the power of
suggestion people can
develop all sorts of
symptoms and also be cured of
them.

SMITH
(looking unimpressed at the man)
Really… If you will excuse me I've just remembered I have something to do.

Smith winks at Polly and walks up on to the platform. Sister May finishes her song and leaves the platform with her brother John. The people are still clapping.

SMITH (CONT'D)
(speaking to the people)
We have been entertaining you today, but at our next healing meeting on Saturday, it will be your turn to entertaining us with your testimonies. Now, who wants to be healed.

Many of the people stand up and cheer and clap again. Smith leaves the platform and goes down to the front to the people.
A large number of them crowd around Smith as he begins to pray for them.

EXT. ON A STREET IN BRADFORD. AFTERNOON.
Smith and the frail lady, he took to the banquet, are walking back to her house.

EXT. OUTSIDE OF HOUSE AT VICTOR ROAD. EARLY EVENING. NEW YEARS DAY. 1913.
Smith as just left his house and is coming down the steps from the front door. Half way down the steps, he is approached by a POLICEMAN and a DOCTOR who talk to him.

POLICEMAN
Mr Wigglesworth.

SMITH
Yes, how can I help you?

POLICEMAN

I'm afraid we have some bad news
for you. It's your wife, sir. She
collapsed at the Mission Hall's
door just as she was leaving.

SMITH

Is she alright.

POLICE DOCTOR

(in a low sad voice)
I'm afraid I have some bad news for
you, sir. She's dead, sir, I was
called to the incident and tried to
revive her. But I'm afraid it was
too late.

Smith drops his bag and raises both arms in the air and shouts
with a loud cry.

SMITH

Hallelujah, Glory to God.

The Policeman and the Doctor look at each other bewildered.

POLICE DOCTOR

(raising his voice again)
But you don't understand, sir, I
said I'm afraid she's dead.
(speaking to the policeman)
He must be in shock. I'll give him
a sedative.

SMITH

But you don't understand, she's
gone to be with the Lord first.

INT. INSIDE OF HOUSE AT VICTOR ROAD. LIVING ROOM. DAYTIME.

Smith's house is full of people who have come to mourn the death of Polly. Smith makes his way from the living room to the upstairs bedroom.

INT. INSIDE THE BEDROOM AT VICTOR ROAD. DAYTIME.

Inside the bedroom, Polly has been laid out on the bed. Smith sits down on the bed next to Polly.

SMITH
(starting to pray in an angry manner)
Lord you know how much I miss
Her… And as hard as I try I just
Can't let her go… I need her so
Much… I just need to tell her how
much I love her again.
(banging his right fist into his left hand)
You can take who you want, I just want my Polly back.

Smith stands up and starts to walk backwards and forwards anxiously. He then puts his right hand on Polly's forehead and prays for her to return back to life.

SMITH (CONT'D)
I rebuked this spirit of death and
commanded that life return to this
body.

After a short while, Polly opens her eyes and smiles at Smith.

POLLY
Smith why have you brought me back
again. You know that I belong to
the Lord now. You must release me
and let me return to him again.

SMITH
(smiling broadly at her)
But I need you so much. I'm so weak
without you.

POLLY
No Smith, the Lord will give you
all the strength you need to carry
on.

Polly closes her eyes and returns to death again.

EXT. NABB WOOD CEMETERY. OUTSKIRTS OF BRADFORD. DAYTIME.

Smith and his family are gathered around Polly's coffin as it is lowered into the ground at the cemetery.

EXT. AT THE SEA FRONT ON ROKER BEACH, SUNDERLAND. THURSDAY MORNING 15 MAY, 1913.

A party of about 25 people are on the beach at Roker. Smith is standing in the sea up to his waist in the freezing cold water. He has just baptized four people in the sea.

Also on the beach are two other men, one a PHOTOGRAPHER with a large camera, and a REPORTER from the Daily Mirror taking notes in a small book.

A YOUNG WOMAN is waiting on the beach for her turn. The rest of the people are singing hymns on the beach.

SMITH
(In a loud roar)
Who's next?

The young woman timidly steps forward into the cold sea to join Smith.

SMITH (CONT'D)
Do you confess your sins and ask
the Lord into your life as your

saviour. Raise your right arm and
say yes I do, if this is so.

YOUNG WOMAN
(raising her right arm)
Yes I do.

SMITH
Then in the name of the Farther,
the Son, and the Holy Ghost, I
baptize you for the remission of
your sins.

Holding onto her head, Smith push's the women backwards
into the sea, and then pulls her up again quickly.

The young woman struggles to make her way out of the water
and on to the beach.

Once on the beach, she collapses into the arms of ANOTHER
WOMAN. Smith also calmly makes his way back to the beach.

DAILY MIRROR REPORTER
(looking puzzled at Smith)
Do you realize just how cold that
water is.

SMITH
Oh yes, but it's better that they
freeze to death in the sea than to
burn in hell.

INT. INSIDE BOWLAND STREET MISSION HALL. MORNING SERVICE.
Smith is on the platform talking to the congregation at the
Sunday morning service.

SMITH
(clearing his throat to speak louder)
Now as some of you may be aware,

God has been directing this ministry
in a new direction. The book of
Mark says, go into all the world
and preach the gospel to every
creature.

 (leaning forward onto the rostrum)
Now that's exactly what I intend to
do with this ministry, to take it
worldwide.

(standing back again)
While I'm away, you will be left in
very good hands.

(turning his head to look at three men sitting behind him)
These dear brothers are quite
capable of looking after the
ministry while I'm gone. I'll be
sailing for Canada and the United
States of America on the 19th of
this month.

END OF ACT TWO

FADE OUT

Act Three

EXT. NIAGARA FALLS. USA, CANADIAN BOARDER. APRIL 1914. DAYTIME.

Smith is standing on the Canadian side of the boarder doing deep breathing exercises when a small party of tourist stop in front of him.

He then overhears a YOUNG TOUR GUIDE talking to a party.

YOUNG TOUR GUIDE
(talking to his group)
The falls were first found by the
Neutral Indians, who named the
falls NIAGARA, which means
thundering water. The Neutral
Indians were the first…

SMITH
(putting his arm around the young tour guide)
Son, let me tell you that the falls
could not have been found by the
Neutral Indians, or anybody else.
God never lost them, he knew they
were here all the time.

Smith patting the young tour guide on the back and walking away.

INT. INSIDE A LARGE MARQUEE ON CAZADERO CAMPSITE. CALIFORNIA USA. EVENING SERVICE.

Smith is standing in front of a platform in the marquee with his jacket off and his sleeves rolled up. There are about two thousand people in front of him.

He has just finished praying for a small group of people. Suddenly an ELDERLY DEAF MAN who Smith has prayed for starts to run up and down the marquee holding both hands over his ears and shouting loudly.

ELDERLY DEAF MAN
What's that noise, what is that?
It's so… Oh my God I can hear.
I can hear, I can hear…

Smith moves forward to catch hold of the man as he runs back towards the platform.

SMITH
(still holding the man)
It's alright, It's alright. Now
tell us what's happened.

ELDERLY DEAF MAN
I can hear, It's amazing, I can hear
again, and the noise is so loud.

Smith holds up the man's hand and the crowd start to cheer.

INT. INSIDE THE HALLWAY AT 70 VICTOR ROAD. FEBRUARY 1915. DAYTIME.

Smith comes through the front door. A telegram for Smith is waiting on a small table in the hallway.

He takes off his hat and coat and hangs them up. He then picks up the telegram and reads it. Stumbling to the bottom of the stairs he sits down with his head in his hands.

SMITH
(looking up and crying out loud)
Oh no, not again Lord, not my son
as well. Why have you done this to
me again?

Dropping the telegram to the floor, it reads, FROM THE WAR OFFICE, SORRY TO INFORM YOU OF THE DEATH OF GEORGE WIGGLESWORTH…

INT. INSIDE BOWLAND STREET MISSION HALL. DAYTIME.
Smith is praying for a YOUNG BOY in a wheelchair. The BOY'S FATHER is next to him on his right side. Smith is also being watched by ANOTHER LOCAL JOURNALIST, who is making notes.

SMITH (CONT'D)
(laying hands on the boy's forehead)
Now son, we are going to ask for
your healing.
(praying with great authority in his voice)
O Lord, just as in the days when
you walked this earth, men were
bound by all kinds of evil spirits. (MORE)

SMITH (CONT'D)
But your power and blood set them free, we ask the
same for this young boy who is bound in this chair. In
your mighty name we ask that this young boy rise up
and walk.

The boy's father looks at Smith in an unimpressed manner.

BOY IN A WHEELCHAIR
(with great excitement)
Father I can feel my legs are
getting warmer and warmer.

The young boy holds on to Smith and his father. He starts to pull himself up from the wheelchair and then slowly starts to walk.

BOY IN A WHEELCHAIR (CONT'D)
Look father I'm walking, I'm
walking.

After a few steps, the boy falls into his father's arms. Smith and the boy's father help him back into the chair.

SMITH
If you believe that God has healed
you, then give him praise and shout
Hallelujah.

BOY IN A WHEELCHAIR
(shouting loudly)
Hallelujah, Hallelujah,
(back to speaking)
I was walking, wasn't I father?

BOY'S FATHER
(in a sceptical manner)
Yes son, you were walking alright.
Now let's take you home.

The father pushes his son away. Smith is then approached by the journalist and a small group of people.

LOCAL JOURNALIST
(with pen and notebook at the ready)
Mr Wigglesworth, this show of
yours, and these clams of great
healings that we have just seen.
Are they not just a little
exaggerated.

SMITH
(in a hard tone)
Certainly not, God doesn't need to
exaggerate, anyway why don't you
ask the people who have just been
healed.

Smith tries to walk away, but the journalist stands in his way
and stops him.

LOCAL JOURNALIST
(in an arrogant manner)
Well, yes I would but anyone can
make clams of healings. There are
those that believe that all these
people who claim to have been
healed, have been brainwashed into
believing they have been made well.

SMITH
(in a sarcastic manner)
O really, how interesting.

Once again Smith tries to walk away and again the journalist
stands in his way.

LOCAL JOURNALIST
One last thing, these stories of
healings that supposedly took
place in America and were
published in Rev. Boddy's news
paper, Confidence. And I quote.
After prayer and the laying on of
hands, she was totally healed. And
you go on to say that she kept the
cancerous growth, in a glass
jar… Now how do you expect my
readers to believe this story.

SMITH
(frown turning to smile)
If you would be so kind as to leave
your address with me, I'll have the
good lady in question send you a
sample of it. Good day to you, sir.

Smith walks away.

INT. INSIDE A MISSION HALL IN CHARTRES, FRANCE. DAYTIME 1920.

Smith is sitting on the front row at the mission hall waiting to go on to the platform and preach.

Sitting next to Smith, is MADAME DEBAT, who is acting as Smith's interpreter.

The congregation is being led in song by a French minister on the platform. A man comes from outside and speaks into Madame Debat's ear. She then turns to Smith and speaks to him.

MADAME DEBAT
(with a strong French ascent)
Messieurs, we must go outside at
once.
(standing up and dragging Smith by the arm)
There is a very sick man who needs
your help immediately.

EXT. OUTSIDE THE MISSION HALL, STILL DAYTIME.

Smith and Madame Debat go outside into the street. Outside on the road is a cart being pulled by two oxen towards the hall.

On the back of the cart is a very sick man lying in a bed of straw and holding a small bag tightly in his right hand.

The cart is also being followed by four men who are talking quietly to themselves.

As the cart stops outside the hall, the man who drove the cart steps down and goes to the back of the cart.

A small group of local village people are also gathered around the cart.

SMITH
(approaching the cart)
What's wrong with him?

MADAME DEBAT
It seems he has a cancer in the
stomach and he is nearly dead.

SMITH
(looking at the man closely)
How long as he been like this.

MADAME DEBAT
(speaking in French to the man who drove the cart)
He is asking how long he has been
ill for.

MAN WHO DROVE THE CART
(shrugging his shoulders and then speaking in French to Madame
Debat)
Who knows, maybe a few months, but
for the last week he is not eating
and getting worse.

MADAME DEBAT
(speaking English to Smith)
For the last week he has been
getting worse and has not eaten.

SMITH
(speaking to Madame Debate)
What's that in his hand?

MADAME DEBAT
(speaking to the man who drove the cart)
He wants to know what's in the
bag.

MAN WHO DROVE THE CART
(speaking to Madame Debate)
That's his food for the return
journey.

MADAME DEBAT
(Speaking to Smith)
That's his food.

SMITH
(speaking to Madame Debate)
I thought you said he had not eaten
for a week.

Madame Debate looks at the man who drove the cart but doesn't speak to him. The man who drove the cart looks back at her and also doesn't speak to her, but shrugs his shoulders once again.

MADAME DEBAT
(speaking to Smith)
I think Messieurs he is expecting
you to heal him and he will be
hungry on his way home.

SMITH
(with a big smile on his face)
Now that's the kind of faith I can
work with.

Smith leans into the back of the cart and pushes his fist into the sick man's stomach and begins to pray for him.

SMITH (CONT'D)
In your holy name Lord God, I
rebuke this spirit sickness, I
command you to leave this man's
body right now.

As Smith takes his hand away from the sick man's stomach, he sits up sharply.

The crowd standing around the cart, jump back in surprise and amazement.

EXT. JUST OUTSIDE THE CITY OF LAUSANNE, NEAR LAKE GENEVA, SWITZERLAND. DAYTIME. 1920.

A car pulls up by the side of the road overlooking Lake Geneva. Smith gets out of the back of the car and stands by the edge of the road looking out across the lake.

SMITH
(breathing deeply in the fresh air and talking to himself)
Oh Lord, such beauty you have
bestowed upon us.

The rear window of the limousine opens and Madame Debate leans out of the car to talk to Smith.

MADAME DEBAT
(in a worrying manner)
Monsieur, monsieur, we must not be
late for the meeting, so many
people are expecting you to come.

SMITH
(turning back to face her)
Yes sister, I'm coming now.
(looking across the lake again and standing with his arms
stretched out wide to form a cross)
(MORE)

SMITH (CONT'D)
Let your spirit fill your people Lord, just as this water
fills this valley.

Smith gets back into the car and it drives off again.

INT. INSIDE A MISSION HALL, LAUSANNE, SWITZERLAND. DAYTIME.

Smith is standing in front of a full congregation of about five hundred people.

Two men come forward from the back helping a BLIND MAN and his SICK WIFE towards Smith.

One of the men speaks to Madame Debate who is standing next to Smith.

MADAME DEBAT
(speaking to SMITH)
This man wants you to pray for his
wife who is dying of tuberculosis.

SMITH
(looking at the man's face and realizing he is blind)
And what does he want for himself.

MADAME DEBAT
He has only asked for prayer for
his wife.

SMITH
Then he will get prayer for his
wife, after I have prayed for him.

Smith moves towards the couple and places his right hand on the blind man's forehead and begins to pray for him.

The man's wife is so sick that she cannot stand up by herself and is being held up by the men helping them.

SMITH (CONT'D)
In the precious name of our Lord
God, I command these eyes to open
and see.

BLIND MAN
(trying to interrupt Smith in French)
No, no. Pray for my wife, she's the
one who's dying.

SMITH
The word of God says that those
who put themselves last shall be
first.

The blind man staggers back slightly and begins to look up
and around him.

BLIND MAN
(speaking softly in French)
I can see light, I can see light
all around me.

The man continues to mumble to himself and is rubbing his
eyes as he is looking around him. Smith then begins to pray for
the man's wife.

SMITH
(putting his hand on her forehead and speaking to Madame
Debat)
Tell this sister that God will heal
her because of her faith.

MADAME DEBAT
(speaking in French to the woman)
He says your faith in God will heal
you.

SMITH
We command healing to this sister's
body in your holy. Amen.

The woman falls backwards but she is caught by the man helping her. Smith beckons the man to bring her closer to him again.

As she comes closer to Smith, she starts to stand on her own.

INT. INSIDE A MISSION HALL IN NEUCHATEL, SWITZERLAND. DAYTIME. 1920.

Smith is standing in front of a congregation of about six hundred people with a WOMEN WEARING A HEAD SCARF to cover her face. Next to her is a YOUNG INTERPRETER talking to Smith.

A large crowd are also outside the building trying to get in.

SMITH
(talking to his interpreter)
(MORE)

SMITH (CONT'D)

Tell her not to be afraid and to trust God and remove her scarf.

YOUNG INTERPRETER
(speaking French to the women)
He says to remove your scarf and
not to be afraid.

The woman removes her scarf to reveal a very large cancerous growth on her face. The congregation make a noise of aghast and surprise.

Smith pulls the woman closer to his side and puts his arm around her and speaks quietly into her ear.

SMITH
Don't be afraid.
(speaking to the interpreter)
Tell them that because of her
faith, she will be healed.

YOUNG INTERPRETER
(speaking French to the congregation)
He says that because of her faith
she will be healed.

SMITH
(placing his hand gently on her forehead)
In the name of our Lord, be healed.
(speaking to the interpreter)
Tell them that when she comes back
tomorrow, she will have a new face.

YOUNG INTERPRETER
He says that her face will be made
new when she comes back tomorrow.

INT. MISSION HALL, ONE HOUR LATER DAYTIME.

The service as just finished and Smith is standing, talking to a small group of people in the mission hall.

He is then approached by a well-dressed man in his fifties, who introduces himself to Smith.

DR EMIL LANZ
(speaking English with a German accent)
(MORE)

DR EMIL LANZ (CONT'D)
Good afternoon to you sir, my name is LANZ, DR
EMIL LANZ.

SMITH
Good afternoon to you, I hope you
enjoyed the service.

DR EMIL LANZ
Yes of cause, most enjoyable. As a
man who has great interest in the
health and well-being of people, I

136

found your clams most interesting.
For example, the healing of sick
bodies and the removal of all
diseases through prayer.

SMITH
Prayer is a powerful weapon against
sickness and disease.

DR EMIL LANZ
I also remember reading your
article on how God healed you and
renewed your body totally after
many years of suffering.

SMITH
Yes that's correct sir.

DR EMIL LANZ
I presume that included your teeth.

SMITH
(with a smile)
Which branch of medicine do you
practice DR LANZ.

DR EMIL LANZ
Dentistry sir, I have a practice in
Berne. I would very much like to
examine your teeth for you sir.

SMITH
Certainly, when I come to Berne I
will come and see you.
DR EMIL LANZ
(pulling up a chair for Smith)
We can do it now, it will only take
a minute.

Smith sits down on the chair. Dr Lanz pulls out an examining tool from his top pocket.

> **DR EMIL LANZ (CONT'D)**
> (looking into Smith mouth)
> Open as wide as you can please. Em…
> em, Oh very good, I can see that
> you must have regular treatment.

> **SMITH**
> On the contrary sir, you are the
> first man to look into my mouth
> since I was a child. Good day to
> you sir.

Smith stands up and walks away.

INT. INSIDE THE MISSION HALL IN NEUCHATEL. DAYTIME.

Once again Smith is standing in front of a packed-full congregation in the mission hall. The young interpreter is also standing next to Smith.

> **SMITH**
> The book of Mark tells us to go
> into all the world and preach the
> gospel to everyone.

At the front row to the left of Smith, a young SCRUFFY LOOKING MAN starts to mimic SMITH every time he speaks.

> **YOUNG INTERPRETER**
> (speaking French to the congregation)
> He says, in the book of Mark, it
> tells us to preach the gospel to
> all the world.

SMITH
(looking at the mimicking young man out the corner of his eye)
He that believeth and is baptized
shall be saved.

The young man continues to mimic SMITH.

YOUNG INTERPRETER
He says, if you believe and are
baptized, you will be saved.

Smith walks over to the mimicking young man and stands in front of him. He then makes a sign for the interpreter not to speak.

SMITH
(looking at the young man)
And these signs shall follow them
that believe, in my name shall they
cast out devils.
(Smith putting his hand on the young man's head)
I command you spirit to leave this
young man in the holy name of our
Lord.

Smith drives out an evil spirit from the young man. He falls to the floor and begins to shake violently for about thirty seconds.

Some of the congregation stand up and move forward towards him. Smith stands over the young man and holds back the congregation from getting too close.

SMITH (CONT'D)
(speaking to the interpreter)
Tell them to remain in their seats.
Give him some air, get back please.

YOUNG INTERPRETER
Please stay in your seats please.

(two men come from the congregation to take the young man) away. The rest of them return to their seats and start to calm down. Smith and the interpreter remain at the front.

SMITH
(raising his arms to silence the crowd)
Now do you really want to see the
power of God's work.

YOUNG INTERPRETER
Do you want to see God's power
work?

A loud shout of yes in French comes back from the crowd. Smith moves off to the side and takes hold of a woman's arm and leads her to the front.

It is the same women from the previous night who had a cancerous growth on her face. She is also wearing a head scarf to cover her face.

SMITH
All those who were here yesterday,
put your hand up.

YOUNG INTERPRETER
Who was here yesterday? Put your
hand up.

About three quarters of the congregation put their hands up.

SMITH
(slowing untying the woman's head scarf)
Don't be afraid my dear.

Smith takes the woman's scarf off to reveal a perfectly healed face. The congregation gasp in disbelief and then a loud roar of praise comes from them.

SMITH (CONT'D)
(shouting loudly)
This is the power of God, look at
her face.

The congregation continue to cheer and clap.

INT. INSIDE GODIVIL POLICE STATION. GODIVIL TOWN CENTRE, SWITZERLAND. 1920. DAYTIME.

Smith is being questioned by a POLICE INSPECTOR who is sitting at a desk. Standing next to Smith are TWO POLICE CONSTABLES and a LOCAL WOMAN.

POLICE INSPECTOR
(speaking English with an accent in a harsh tone)
Monsieur, this is the second
complaint I've had against you
since you've been in this country.
(showing Smith a letter)
Look at this. It is signed by some
of this country's leading doctors.
They complain that you are
unqualified to do this work and
that you are healing sick people
without a licence.
(showing Smith a second letter)
Look at this, it is from Church
Ministers. They say that what you
are doing is by demonic powers.
(holding another piece of paper and speaking softer)
(MORE)

POLICE INSPECTOR (CONT'D)
However, I also have a written testimony from
MADAME here, claiming to have been cured of her
drunkenness and bad behaviour when you prayed for
her.

WOMAN WITH SMITH
(nodding in agreement and speaking English with an accent)
It is true monsieur.

POLICE INSPECTOR
And my men can also testify that
her behaviour was indeed bad. She
has spent many nights in my cells
in a drunken state.

The two police constables also nod in agreement.

POLICE INSPECTOR (CONT'D)
So in light of this I am prepared
to allow you to continue, but only
on the condition that there are no
more complains. Do I make myself
clear monsieur?

SMITH
O yes, you have made yourself quite
clear Inspector.

EXT. THE FJORDS OUTSIDE BERGEN, NORWAY. 1921. DAYTIME.
Smith and a fellow minister, THOMAS BARRATT are
walking by the side of the fjords talking to each other.

SMITH
I want to thank you Thomas for
agreeing to interpret for me.

THOMAS BARRATT
(speaking English to Smith with a Norwegian accent)
It's my pleasure, I'm happy to
help. I think you will like Bergen,
it's a nice quite little town.

EXT. ON A ROAD TRAVELLING TO BERGEN TOWN CENTRE. DAYTIME.

Smith and Thomas are sitting in the back of a car being driven by a Chauffeur to a mission hall.

When the car is about two miles from the mission hall, they both notice that hundreds of people are walking in the same direction as them.

Many sick people are also being pushed along the road in push chairs. Further on, they start to hear a loud noise coming from the mission hall.

THOMAS BARRATT
(speaker to the Chauffeur in Norwegian)
Stop the car a moment please.

The car stops.

THOMAS BARRATT (CONT'D)
(speaking to Smith in English)
This is strange, I have never heard
this noise before.

SMITH
(putting his head out of the window to hear clearer)
It sounds like a loud roar of the
wind.

THOMAS BARRATT
Yes, or a train, but we are too far
from the station.
(speaking to the Chauffeur again)
OK, let's move on.

The car moves on and approaches the mission hall. Smith and Thomas realize where the noise was coming from.

In the streets there are thousands of people pushing and shoving each other and trying to get into the hall.

The noise from the crowd is very loud, and there are several police officers on horseback trying to control the crowds of people.

Smith's car is unable to drive any closer to the hall. Both men get out of the car and try to walk to the hall, but because of the crowd they can't move.

Thomas grabs a POLICE OFFICER by the arm and speaks to him.

THOMAS BARRATT (CONT'D)
(shouting loud in Norwegian to the officer)
(MORE)

THOMAS BARRATT (CONT'D)
We must get through to the hall.
(pointing to Smith)
This man is leading the service.

The police officer speaks to a group of his colleagues. They then help them push their way towards the mission hall.

THOMAS BARRATT (CONT'D)
(grabbing Smith's arm)
We need to follow them.

About one hundred yards from the building, Thomas lets go of Smith's arm.

Smith then stops and leans through the back window of a car which is caught up in the traffic jam. On the back seat, a SICK WOMAN is lying down with her eyes closed.

A SMALL BOY and GIRL are lying next to her, they are both crying. The WOMAN'S HUSBAND is sitting in the driver's seat with his body turned around trying to comfort them.

SMITH
(speaking to the HUSBAND in slow English)
What is wrong with her?

SICK WOMAN'S HUSBAND
(answering back in English with a Norwegian accent)
She is dying of a cancer, it is
inside of her stomach.

Smith opens the rear door of the car and leans inside. He then pushes his right hand fist into the woman's stomach and begins to pray for her.

SMITH
I rebuke this sickness. Be gone and
leave this woman's body right now.

The woman sits up sharply and lets out a loud sigh, she then starts to breathe very heavy. Her husband reaches out his hand and takes hold of her hand.

The women then starts to breathe normally. She opens her eyes and smiles at her husband, and the children stop crying.

The husband then starts to cry tears of joy as his wife sits up straight in the back seat of the car.

SICK WOMAN'S HUSBAND
(grabbing Smith's hand and shaking it very hard)
(MORE)

SICK WOMAN'S HUSBAND (CONT'D)
Thank you, thank you very much for saving my wife.
Thank you.

Smith then carries on walking towards the hall. Thomas makes his way to the building entrance and turns around looking for Smith.

Smith puts up his arm to signal that he is alright. A few yards further up the road, Smith stops next to a woman carrying a crying baby.

SMITH
(laying hands on the baby's forehead)
Oh Lord, we command in your
precious name that this child be
healed.

The baby stops crying and Smith moves on further down the road. Again he stops and looks into the cars in the traffic jam and starts to pray for the sick people in them.

Cries of joy from the healed people can be heard coming from several of the cars. As Smith moves on, some people from the crowd realize who he is and mob him.

Smith is then pushed to the ground, but he is rescued by TWO POLICEMAN who come back for him and help him to the building.

EXT. OPEN AIR PARK. STOCKHOLM, SWEDEN. APRIL 1921. DAYTIME.

Smith is standing on a large platform in the park. In front of him are twenty thousand people in the congregation.

SMITH
(speaking to a SWEDISH INTERPRETER)
Certain people complained to your
Government and tried to have me
removed from this country.

SWEDISH INTERPRETER
(speaking Swedish to the congregation)
He says that the Government wanted
to remove him from Sweden.

SMITH
But your King, His Majesty allowed
me to stay. On one condition, that
I must not lay hands or touch
anyone in prayer.

SWEDISH INTERPRETER
His Majesty has allowed him to stay
in Sweden. But he must not lay
hands on you at all.

SMITH
But God has told me that if you want
to be healed, to lay hands on
yourself and you will be healed.

SWEDISH INTERPRETER
He says that God as told him to
tell you to lay hands on yourself
and pray for your own healing.

Thousands of people in the congregation are laying hands on their selves and are being healed.

INT. INSIDE A CHURCH IN COLOMBO, CEYLON. (SRI LANKA) DAYTIME.

The church is full with hundreds of people inside. There are also many hundreds of them waiting outside trying to get in.

Smith is standing in front of the congregation. He as just asked for all the sick crying baby to be brought forward in a line by their mothers.

SMITH
(walking along the line)
I rebuke the sickness in these
children in the name of our Lord.

As he lays hands on them, they stop crying and their mothers take them away.

And then a blind man is brought forward for prayer and Smith lays hands on him and prays for him.

SMITH (CONT'D)
(holding his right hand across the man's eyes)
Heal these eyes Lord, we command
this in your holy name.

Almost immediately the man is healed and cries out with joy.

HEALED MAN
I can see. Thank you for healing
me. I can see, I can see…

Suddenly many sick people from the congregation surge forward and grab hold of Smith, as they do so many of them are healed.

The MINISTER of the church and some helpers rescue Smith and lead him away into a side room. Bolting the door behind them.

Cries of joy can be heard from the crowd the other side of the door.

HELPING MINISTER
(looking amazed at what he has just seen)
I've never seen anything like that
in my life before. All those sick
people who touched you were healed.
It's unbelievable.

SMITH
No, the key to being healed is
belief. If you believe enough, then
you will be healed.

INT. A BAPTIST CHURCH, SYDNEY, AUSTRALIA. 1922. DAYTIME.
Smith is standing in front of the platform next to a WOMAN IN A WHEEL CHAIR. Smith holds up the woman to make her stand against her wishes.

SMITH

If you want to walk again, first
you must stand.

WOMAN IN THE WHEEL CHAIR

No I can't, I'm frightened I'll
fall.

SMITH

If you want to walk, you must step
out in faith first.

The woman doesn't move, so Smith pushes her in the back to make her walk.

The congregation can't believe what they see and gasp at the sight of Smith pushing her to walk.

First, the woman stumbles forward, but then she starts to walk slowly.

The Congregation start to applaud as she continues to walk.

INT. INSIDE THE WIRTH'S OLYMPIA HALL. MELBOURNE. AUSTRALIA. EARLY EVENING.

Smith is standing on a huge platform about six feet high in front of a packed out hall.

He has just finished preaching and asked for the sick to come forward for prayer. As he moves towards the edge of the platform, he slips and falls off.

Landing on his feet with his arms waving from side to side, he falls into the arms of a man standing in the aisle.

MAN IN THE AISLE

(holding on to Smith)
You've healed my shoulder.
(hugging Smith with delight)
When you touched my shoulder, all
the pain I had in it went. Thank
you brother, thank you.

The man turns towards the congregation and weaves his arms as they cheer and clap him.

EXT. ON THE QUAYSIDE. WELLINGTON HARBOUR, NEW ZEALAND. MAY 1922, DAYTIME.

Smith and several other passengers are getting off a ship. As Smith walks along the quayside, he walks passed a sign which reads welcome to New Zealand.

Just up ahead of Smith, a HARBOUR OFFICIAL can be heard shouting out instructions to the passengers.

> ### HARBOUR OFFICIAL
> (giving direction with his hands)
> This way please ladies and
> gentlemen. Please have all your
> travel documents ready for
> inspection, thank you.

INT. INSIDE WELLINGTON TOWN HALL, BACK OFFICE. EVENING TIME.

The town hall is packed with people waiting for the meeting to start. Smith is sitting in the back office with his back to the door reading a letter.

His friend, HARRY ROBERTS, enters the room with two newspapers in his hand and starts to read one of them to Smith.

> ### HARRY ROBERTS
> (with great enthusiasm in his voice)
> Listen to this, the headline is
> 'Faith Healing, Extraordinary Scenes
> at the Town Hall.'
> (looking up at Smith in surprise)
> Where's your moustache gone.

> ### SMITH
> (continuing to read his letter)
> A long story, I'll tell you later.

HARRY ROBERTS
(continues reading)
E E Pennington who was chairman of
the New Zealand Evangelical
Mission, says…
(mumbling to himself)
And then it says his message was
truly wonderful.
(mumbling to himself again)
And it gives a list of people who
received healing at the meetings so
far.

SMITH
O, very nice.

HARRY ROBERTS
(reading the second newspaper)
Are you listening Smith.

SMITH
Yes, yes, go on.

HARRY ROBERTS
There's another article in this
paper that's not so kind.

SMITH
(still reading his letter)
What does it say?

HARRY ROBERTS
The headline is fact or fiction.
Then it goes on to tell the stories
of a Mrs E Jones and a Mr A Cook
who were prayed for and had hands
laid on them by Mr Wigglesworth
with no effect. And when questioned

why they had not received healing,
they were told that it was probably
because of their lack of faith.
(looking at Smith again)
What are you reading?

SMITH
(showing Harry his letter)
Take a look at this.

HARRY ROBERTS
(taking the letter)
What's in it?

SMITH
It seems I've lost control of my
Mission hall back home in Bradford.

HARRY ROBERTS
They can't do that, can they.

SMITH
Unfortunately they have. Come on,
let's see what's in store for us
now.

They both leave the office and go into the main hall.

EXT. ON BOARD A SHIP MOORED AT FIJI HARBOUR. MID-MORNING. 1923.

Smith is standing on the top deck of a ship leaning against the rail, stroking his moustache.

As he looks across the harbour, a man who is limping badly is being helped back to the ship by a LOCAL MAN.

LOCAL MAN
(looking up at Smith)
Where's the ship's doctor. This man

has been bitten by a snake.

SMITH
(shouting back down)
Wait there, I'm on my way down.

INT. INSIDE OF A SHIP'S CABIN. MID-MORNING.
The MAN WHO WAS BITTEN by a snake is sitting on a cabin bed. His right trousers' leg is rolled up, and he is showing Smith his badly swollen leg.

MAN BITTEN BY SNAKE
(grabbing hold of Smith in a state of panic)
You must help me doctor, I'm dying.
Look at my leg.

SMITH
I'm not a doctor.

MAN BITTEN BY SNAKE
You're not a doctor.

SMITH
No, but I can help you.

MAN BITTEN BY SNAKE
But who are you?

SMITH
I'm just a passenger like you.
(pushing his fist into the bitten area)
I command this poison to leave this
leg and to be healed in the name of
our Lord.

The man's leg starts to heal. The man and the local man look on in amazement. Just then, there is a knock on the door and the SHIP'S DOCTOR enters the cabin.

SHIP'S DOCTOR
I'm told there's a passenger who
was bitten by a poisonous snake.

MAN BITTEN BY SNAKE
That's me.
(showing the doctor his leg)
But look at it now, it's healed.

SHIP'S DOCTOR
(looking at the leg)
It could not have been a poisonous
snake or you would have been dead
by now.

LOCAL MAN
But the snake was poisonous, I
killed it myself.
(pointing at Smith)
Then this man prayed for him and
his leg was healed.

SHIP'S DOCTOR
But that's impossible sir.

SMITH
On the contrary sir, read the Book
of Acts. The Apostle Paul was
bitten by a poisonous snake and he
didn't die.

EXT. ON THE PLATFORM OF BOMBAY STATION, INDIAN. MIDDAY.

Smith is getting off a train when he is mobbed by a large
crowd of people.

Again many people try to touch Smith, and he has to be
rescued by the station master and his staff.

Smith and two of his travelling companions are led into a waiting car and then driven off.

The station master, who touched Smith several times, notices that a painful irritable rash he had on the back of his hand has gone.

INT. INSIDE OF SMITH'S BEDROOM AT 70 VICTOR ROAD. DAYTIME.

Smith is being helped out of bed by his daughter Alice and her husband JAMES.

JAMES
I still think you're not well
enough to get up yet.

SMITH
No, no, I'm alright. God spoke to me
while I was sick. He told me he
would raise me up again and give me
fifteen more years… The forces of
evil are about to be unleashed on
the world and we must be ready to
meet them.

INT. INSIDE A BEDROOM OF A LARGE HOUSE IN LONDON. EARLY EVENING.

Smith is in a large bedroom of a house. A YOUNG TEENAGE GIRL who is possessed by evil spirits is being held down to the floor by FIVE MEN.

POSSESSED GIRL
(screaming at Smith in a deep voice)
We know who you are, we are too
many for you to cast out.

Smith approaches the young girl and puts his hand on her forehead and speaks for her.

SMITH
(with great authority in his voice)
I know you are many, but you need
to know that he that is in me is
greater than he that is in the
world, your master. And by this
power, that is in me, I command you
to leave this young girl. In the
name of our Lord be gone.

The girl pulls herself free from the men holding her and begins to cough out evil spirits.

The men look on in horror and amazement as the spirits leave her body one by one snarling at Smith as they disappear in the air.

INT. INSIDE THE LIVING ROOM OF THE HOUSE. EARLY MORNING.

Smith, the GIRL and her PARENTS are sitting around a table together.

SMITH
Over the years, I have learnt that
giving praise and thanks to God
will always move His Spirit. And
sometimes, it will even move the
spirit of the evil one.

INT. INSIDE OF SMITH'S BEDROOM. NIGHT TIME.

Smith is suddenly awoken in the middle of the night. As he turns over to look into the corner of the room, a DARK FIGURE with red eyes is standing there.

SMITH
(sitting up in bed)
Oh it's you, what on earth do you
want at this hour.
(Shaking his head in disbelief and lying down again.)

DARK FIGURE
Fool, this foolish nonsense of
mankind.

SMITH
(sitting up sharply)
Foolish nonsense, how dare you
speak of that. You who was created
beautiful and perfect in every way,
and stood at his right hand side.
You gave it all up out of pride and
greed, to become this…
(Smith gestures with his hand)
…And he still calls you
Lucifer, doesn't that tell you
anything… I've no time for this,
I need my sleep, being a mere
mortal.

Smith then lays down and goes back to sleep again.

EXT. ON THE REAR DECK OF AN OCEAN LINER. DAYTIME. 1936.

Smith is being helped back to his cabin by his daughter Alice and his son-in-law, James.

SMITH
I'm so much looking forward to this
trip, I've been told that the
people of Africa have great faith.

INT. INSIDE OF TOWN HALL, CAPE TOWN, SOUTH AFRICA. EVENING TIME.

Smith is standing in front of the platform praying for a large group of people from the congregation.

Standing around him are Alice and James and a South African Minister named DAVID du PLESSIS. Smith then signals to James to help him.

JAMES
(holding onto Smith)
Are you alright?

SMITH
Help me back to the hotel, I'm in
some pain with my leg and I need to
rest it.

James signals to Alice to carry on praying for the people.
David du Plessis approaches the two men to see if everything is
alright.

DAVID DU PLESSIS
Is everything alright?

SMITH
Yes I'm fine, I'm feeling a little
tied, I just need to lay down for a
while.
INT. INSIDE THE REAR OF A CAR. EVENING TIME.
Smith and James are sitting in the rear seats of the car
travelling back to their hotel.

SMITH
I have a bad rupture, it causes me
great pain if I stand for too long.

JAMES
Then we must cancel the trip and
return home and see a doctor.

SMITH
No, no, we must stay and do God's
work, I'll be alright once I've had
some rest.

EXT. THE VELD, GRASSLANDS OF SOUTH AFRICA. DAYTIME.

Smith is travelling in a car with Alice and James across the Veld in South Africa. Sitting next to the driver in the front passenger seat is a SOUTH AFRICAN INTERPRETER.

EXT. A ZULU VILLAGE IN SOUTH AFRICA. DAYTIME.

Smith is speaking to about two hundred villagers through the interpreter in their village.

INT. INSIDE THE OFFICE OF DAVID DU PLESSIS. JOHANNESBURG. EARLY MORNING.

David du Plessis is sitting at his desk, writing some notes. Smith enters into the room without knocking on the door and grabs David by the hand and leads him into the corridor.

INT. THE CORRIDOR OUTSIDE DAVID'S OFFICE. EARLY MORNING.

Outside in the corridor, Smith pushes David against the wall and pins him to it.

SMITH

God has given me a message for you David. He wants you to know that an amazing revival will soon take place. You will be so involved in it that you will become known as Mr Pentecostal.

Smith releases David and walks away.

INT. PRESTON EASTER CONVENTION. MORNING SERVICE. 1945.

Smith is on the platform in front of a large congregation. Alice and James are sitting behind him.

SMITH
(opening his Bible)
My reading this morning is from
Romans 8:11. But if the spirit of
him that raised up Jesus from the
dead dwell in you, he that raised
up Christ from the dead shall also
quicken your mortal bodies by his
spirit that dwelleth in you…
(closing his Bible and talking to the congregation)
Many times in my life I have been
laid up with terrible sickness.
Sometimes in secret, sometimes not.
I have been so bad that I thought I
would die. I was even ready to meet
the Lord. But by his hand, he raised
me up and I asked why? Why save me
now, has not my time come yet Lord?
And he answered me no, you are my
testimony. Tell my people of my
goodness and I will raised them
up, they that believe in me.

INT. INSIDE THE LIVING ROOM AT VICTOR ROAD. DAYTIME. 1945.

Smith and James are standing in the living room looking out of the window onto the street. A parade has marched past to celebrate the end of the Second World War.

JAMES
Well, at last that madness is over.

SMITH
That's exactly what you get when
you step out of line from the will
of God.

JAMES
What's that?

SMITH
Madness, total madness.

INT. INSIDE A HOSPITAL WARD. DAYTIME. 1947.
Smith is sitting by the bed of WILFRED RICHARDSON who is recovering in hospital after a major operation.

WILFRED RICHARDSON
I've preached divine healing
through faith for many years now...
And now I find myself in hospital
recovering from an operation.
(shaking his head from side to side)
What will they say?

SMITH
(placing his hand on Wilfred's hand to comfort him)
The important thing is that God
will understand. He has a plan for
our lives and many people including
Christians, fight against it.

END OF FLASH BACK PRESENT TIME. MARCH 12. 1947. DAYTIME. SERIES OF SHOTS.

1. INT. INSIDE SMITH'S CAR.
2. EXT. OUTSIDE OF CHURCH.
3. INT. INSIDE OF CHURCH.
4. INT. INSIDE THE VESTRY.

The car is about two hundred yards from the Church as Smith finishes talking to the Greens.

As the car stops at the church, organ music can be heard coming from inside. Smith and the Greens get out of the car and enter the building.

Inside the church, Smith and Alfred Green walk past a full congregation in the sanctuary. Mrs Green takes a seat, while the two men enter into the vestry.

As Smith and Green enter into the vestry, ELDER HIBBERT and TWO OTHER MEN are warming themselves up by an open coal fire.

All the men greet each other with handshakes. James enters the vestry and gives Smith a hug. Smith and Elder Hibbert then stand aside and begin a conversation of their own.

ELDER HIBBERT
(rubbing his hands to stay warm)
At lease it's a bit warmer than
yesterday. And a good turnout.

SMITH
(also rubbing his hands)
Yes a full house. How's that
daughter of yours doing.

ELDER HIBBERT
(looking a little disappointed)
She says she feels a little better
since you prayed for her.

SMITH
Tell her to believe then God will
heal her.

Smith then falls forward into Elder Hibbert's arms. Hibbert calls out to the others for help.

ELDER HIBBERT
Help me, Smith has fallen over and
I can't hold him up.

They all rush to help Hibbert hold up Smith but they are unable to do so as Smith is lowered to the floor.

James and the others try to revive him but soon realize that he is dead.

JAMES
(with a shocked look on his face and looking at the others)
My Lord I don't believe it… Has
he really gone from us…

FADE OUT

THE END